An Illustrated Dictionary of Word Processing

by Larry Langman

An Illustrated Dictionary of Word Processing

by Larry Langman

 ORYX PRESS
1986

The rare Arabian Oryx is believed to have inspired the myth of the unicorn. This desert antelope became virtually extinct in the early 1960s. At that time several groups of international conservationists arranged to have 9 animals sent to the Phoenix Zoo to be the nucleus of a captive breeding herd. Today the Oryx population is over 400, and herds have been returned to reserves in Israel, Jordan, and Oman.

Copyright © 1986 by
The Oryx Press
2214 North Central at Encanto
Phoenix, AZ 85004-1483

Published simultaneously in Canada

Printed and Bound in the United States of America

∞ The paper used in this publication meets the minimum requirements of American National Standard for Information Science—Permanence of Paper for Printed Library Materials, ANSI Z39.48, 1984.

Library of Congress Cataloging-in-Publication Data

Langman, Larry.
    An illustrated dictionary of word processing.
    1. Word processing—Dictionaries. I. Title.
Z52.25.L36 1986   652.5′0321   85-43344
ISBN 0-89774-286-9

Table of Contents

Preface

A method of on-screen printout preview to gauge page breaks, heading placement, and similar formatted appearances is provided, but there is no unformatted draft copy or storing of a formatted text file to disk for later printing or data transmissions.
Creative Computing, June 1983

WRITE also uses embedded print-formatting commands, which can be placed anywhere in the text. Write's Editor ignores these commands; they're used only when you print.
Popular Computing, January 1984

The Final Word has a powerful advanced-formatting facility that can be invoked through an advanced-print command. You can embed any number of special formatting commands in the text to obtain perfect formal output arranged spatially and typographically.
Byte, May 1983

The above references, as you may have already guessed, have been culled from magazine reviews of word processors. Other periodicals are not immune from this type of abstruse writing. A recent issue of PC Magazine presented a series of charts containing all the major features of 18 word processors. Two columns of the charts, with the headings "Can chain documents for printing" and "Can queue documents for printing," were followed by either a "yes" or "no" next to each product--with no further explanation of the two terms, either in the charts or in the preceding text. It would be interesting to learn how many readers are still scurrying about trying to distinguish between "chain" and "queue."

One of the purposes of this book is to bring some semblance of order to the terminology buffeted about in the chaotic world of word processing. The publishers of word processing software, the reviewers who write about the programs, and the salespeople who plug some products while shunning others--all use terminology that is more often confusing and intimidating than informative and clarifying.

The truth is that most consumers--even those who may use WPs on a frequent basis--don't understand the hundreds of arcane terms applied to this relatively new area known as word processing. An Illustrated Dictionary of Word Processing, the only comprehensive book in the field, has been designed to clarify this terminology for beginners, for casual users, and for those who are proficient in word processing.

Another purpose of this book is to make word processing fun. This can only be accomplished after the user discovers and understands the many features of a specific WP. Burdensome tasks, such as adding or deleting paragraphs, centering lines, or placing headers and page numbers on each page, require little effort and produce professional results once the intricacies of the WP are learned.

Before long, users find themselves eager to return to the keyboard and face the video screen.

What Is a Word Processor?

The term "word processor" may refer to the hardware and/or software which permits text to be electronically manipulated, corrected, and reproduced. WP hardware consists of a keyboard-operated terminal, a video display, and a magnetic storage device. A computer specifically designed for word processing is called a dedicated word processor. WP software consists of two parts: a text editor and a text formatter. In this book, when the term "word processor" or WP is used, it generally refers to software.

How Does a Word Processor Work?

To learn how a WP does what it is supposed to do, we first have to examine a computer more closely. Every computer contains three elements: a central processing unit (CPU), a memory system, and an input/output (I/O) method for entering data into and obtaining results from the computer. An alphanumeric keyboard, similar to a typewriter, is used as an input device, and a video monitor serves as an output device.

When a software program, such as a WP, is inserted into a disk drive and "booted up," it is read and stored into the computer memory. The CPU, which acts as the "brain" of the computer, manages the memory and executes all the functions that follow. When the user gives instructions, which are entered from the keyboard (the input device), the CPU retrieves the information from its location in memory and carries out the task. The instructions may be a search-and-replace, scroll, or save-to-disk function, the last of which activates an

output device such as a disk drive. When text
entry and editing are completed and the computer is turned off, the WP program that was
temporarily stored in its memory will be lost.
It will, of course, still exist on disk. Also,
any text that was entered on screen and not
saved will be lost. The computer is now ready
to accept another program such as a database
or the WP can be booted up again.

What Does a Word Processor Do?

Word processors (or WPs) can manipulate
and store text. These two features set them
apart from conventional typewriters. With a WP
you don't have to retype an entire page because of a few errors; you can edit, revise,
and review your text on screen before you
commit it to paper. Then, only after you are
completely satisfied with the contents and the
format, you can print the final draft and
store the document on disk for later use or
reference.

All WPs perform two general functions,
text editing and text formatting. Text editing
consists of adding, deleting, and moving
around words on screen to improve the text. To
execute these tasks, different programs offer
different methods, but the results are the
same. Some provide more sophisticated features
such as moving large blocks of text; searching
for, and replacing, words and phrases; or
checking for spelling errors.

The second major function, text formatting, is concerned with how the document will
appear on paper. This includes, for example,
margins, indentations, line spacing, headings,
and page numbers. Again, the more costly WPs
offer a wider array of features such as the
use of footnotes, line centering, and on-
screen formatting--what you see on screen is
what you get on the printed page.

The Word Processor and the Printer

Besides performing text editing and formatting, the WP can handle many other tasks, depending on the printer you choose. You can add underlining, boldface, italics, subscripts, and superscripts. You can print multiple copies, make a draft copy for proofreading before printing a final version, print your document while you edit another, etc.

You can program your WP in conjunction with your printer to print continuous pages, each automatically numbered and containing a header. You can utilize a tractor feed which handles continuous fanfold paper or a single-sheet feeder which automatically loads one page at a time into the printer. Some machines include a tractor feed mechanism; a single-sheet feeder is usually an optional accessory. Many WPs provide utility programs for both of the above procedures.

Various kinds of printers are available, each tailored to the specific needs of the user. For example, dot-matrix printers can help you create graphs and charts that can be entered into your text; daisy wheel printers, which generally operate more slowly, will produce letter-quality printing indistinguishable from that of the best typewriters. If your pocketbook can afford it, you can purchase a laser printer that works more quietly and much faster than the dot-matrix or daisy wheel printers and still produces excellent results.

Selecting a Word Processor

Another purpose of this book is to help you select a WP that suits your needs. Understanding the terminology of WPs can assist you in making the proper choice. Do you need to merge files while editing? Do you want a split-screen function in which you can simul-

taneously edit two documents or parts of the
same one? Will right or full justification
help you in your written presentations? Some
WPs provide automatic tables of contents and
indexes, multiple headers and footers, automatic hyphenation, proportional spacing, and
mailing list merging, as well as other unusual
features. Clearly, the more acquainted you
become with WP language, the better your
chances will be in selecting the right software. Appendix A reviews and evaluates a number of software programs. Appendix B provides
a list of sources for further information.

How to Use This Book

If you are a beginner at word processing,
you should skim through this volume to get a
general idea of the different terms and subjects that are covered. If you are ready to
buy a WP, you will find the book useful in its
definitions of the unfamiliar terminology
appearing in the brochures or advertisements
of the products you are considering. The entries will provide you with clear, up-to-date,
detailed information. If you have been working
with a WP, you can use the book to reacquaint
yourself with some functions, procedures, and
features, as well as familiarize yourself with
other WPs and peripherals. The book can also
be used to supplement the documentation accompanying your program. If the documentation
does not cover a topic sufficiently, check the
entry in this dictionary, as well as the co-
pious cross-references that guide you to further information or related topics. The
writers of the WP manual may have assumed that
the reader is familiar with the term or that
their explanation is satisfactory.
Several frequently used acronyms mentioned in entries are defined within their own
entries. These are: DOS (disk operating system), RAM (Random Access Memory), ROM (Read

Only Memory), and WP (word processor).

Some readers may feel that inclusion of such topics as modems, paper feeders, and technical terms relating to computer processing is straying from the subject of word processing. These entries were included for two reasons: Users of WPs often expand their interests and their hardware into these areas; and these subjects are frequently discussed and written about in conjunction with WPs.

The author would like to thank computer consultant Carmine Ferraro for his suggestions, Spencer Fisher for his editorial help, and Arthur H. Stickney for the concept of this book.

A

Abort
A command used with some WPs such as XYWrite
to delete text in the computer's memory.
Abort, in effect, erases everything that has
been entered since the last save command. <u>See</u>
<u>also</u> Clear.

Access time
The speed at which a system can select data
from its own storage device.

Accessing
A procedure for entering information into or
taking information out of a computer.

Acoustic coupler
A device that connects a modem to a telephone.
The acoustic coupler provides a simple and
inexpensive connection in which one part containing a small speaker is hooked up to the
microphone portion of the telephone and
another part containing a microphone is connected to the speaker half of the telephone. A
more sophisticated connection is the direct-
coupled modem. <u>See</u> <u>also</u> Modem.

Adding files. <u>See</u> Joining text files.

Advanced formatting/printing mode

The ability of a WP to accept embedded formatting commands into text for arranging chapter headings, subheadings, cross-references, indented listings, indexes, and similar items. WPs such as WordStar and Final Word offer a wide array of embedded commands. Usually, the more sophisticated the WP, the more features available and the more time required to learn all the command codes. Advanced formatting offers two advantages in the arrangement of the final text. The user does not have to resort to limited submenus to select some of these functions, and more important, a wider range of these functions can be provided.

Figure A.1 An Embedded Command
for a Header

(as it appears on screen)

.TL ADVENTURES IN WORD PROCESSING

(as it appears in print)

ADVENTURES IN WORD PROCESSING

Align

To position text within margins. Ordinarily, text is aligned automatically according to preset, or default, margins. However, if these margins are changed, the text will be rearranged to conform to the new parameters. Virtually all WPs offer some type of procedure for aligning text. See also Format, Format command, Format file, Text alignment.

Figure A.2   Aligning Text to New Margins

(text within old margins)

Margins are usually set before any
text is entered through a WP program.
Sometimes, however, the user may prefer
to change these margins. This means
that the text must be re-aligned.

(text aligned to new margins)

Margins are usually set
before any text is entered
through a WP program. Sometimes, however, the user may
prefer to change these margins.
This means that the text must
be re-aligned.

Align numbers
A WP command which positions numbers in various ways. Numbers can be aligned and justified
to the left, to the right, or at a specific
decimal point. Usually alignment depends on
the placement of the cursor. In the following
examples the numbers are aligned by decimal
point.

Figure A.3   Aligning Numbers

---

before alignment	after alignment
17.6	17.6
43.32	43.32
2.697	2.697
878	878

Alignment marker
A method of protecting portions of text from
alignment. With some WPs, text requires additional alignment after it has been altered.
However, segments of that text such as charts,
centered lines, and tables may not require
alignment. Alignment markers (sometimes called
alignment protection markers), therefore, are
placed at the beginning and end of the text to
be protected from the alignment function.

Alignment protection. <u>See</u> Alignment marker.

Alphabetical indexing
A sorting feature of a WP. There are two
approaches to alphabetical listing:
"flagging," in which entries are flagged or
stopped within the text itself; and keyboard
entry, in which an index file is created by
typing in each entry. The file is sorted and
finally printed in index format. <u>See</u> <u>also</u>
Index.

Alphanumeric keys
The letter and number keys in the center of a
keyboard, commonly known as the typewriter
keys. With many WP programs, alphanumeric keys
are used to type text or to perform various
functions when combined with the control or
alternate keys. For example, the "l" or "s"
key may be combined with the control key to
execute the load or save command, in which
case no "l" or "s" would appear on screen.

Alternate page numbers
A print format feature of some WPs which enters page numbers on alternate left and right
sides of pages. Some printed documents may
have to meet particular publishing standards,
especially if the work is to be submitted
"camera ready." This means that some companies may request that even numbers appear on
the left side of a page and odd numbers on the

right side, a standard procedure in the printing of books.

Alternate pitch
The ability of a WP to produce more than one
pitch on a line of text or one that is different from the default pitch. The standard
pitch of most WPs is 10 cpi (characters per
inch). Alternate pitch may vary from five to
17 cpi, depending on the program and the capabilities of the printer. See also CPI, Pitch.

Alternating header and footer
A feature of some WPs which permits alternate
headers and footers, e.g., page numbers and/or
text, to be placed on the top or bottom of
each page. Most WPs allow the user to place
information at the top and bottom of each
electronic page. However, in this case, the
program cannot distinguish between odd- and
even-numbered pages, and information will
appear in the same position on each page
(right, left, or center). But sometimes, different data are required on odd-numbered pages
from those appearing on even-numbered pages.
For instance, book manuscripts may require the
title of the work to appear on the left or
even-numbered page and the chapter heading on
the right or odd-numbered page. Some WPs feature alternating headers and footers as well
as different margin settings for odd and even
pages.

Ampersand
The "&" symbol used in some WPs to signify
that the program is in a particular formatting
mode. Ampersand commands are usually embedded,
appearing on screen but not in the printed
document.

Any-length character
A character that can represent a character
string of any length. Any-length characters

are used to find words, dates, names, or any other items in a document. If, for example, a check of all the spellings of the names Caruthers, Crothers, and so on is desired in a list or document, this feature will find each occurrence as well as other strings with similar beginnings and endings. See also Character string, Search and replace.

Figure A.4   Example of Any-length Character

```
                    Find: C#ers

                (screen will display)

        Caruthers              Carothers
        Crothers               Chalmers
```

Appending files
The ability of a WP to attach one or more files on disk to another file in memory. Files that are appended are added to the end of an on-screen file and are permanently merged. This differs from Link Files, which temporarily connects files for special purposes such as search, replace, etc. See also Joining text files.

Applications software
A program that performs a specific task such as word processing, accounting, finance, record keeping, inventory, problem solving, etc. Applications programs are not related to the internal operations of the computer or peripheral devices. These functions, such as helping to run DOS, a modem, and so on, are controlled by systems programs. See also Software.

Arrow key
A keyboard function which controls the movement of the cursor one character or line at a time. Usually the left and right arrow keys move the cursor backward and forward, respectively, while the up and down arrow keys manipulate the cursor up and down one line. Many WPs combine the arrow keys with the control key to move the cursor more than one character, e.g., a word or line at a time. The arrangement of the four arrow keys depends upon the computer manufacturer. The two basic layouts are the horizontal in-line utilized by the Apple IIe and similar models and the diamond cluster on the IBM and similar keyboards. See also Compass layout.

ASCII code
A command signal transmitted by a computer to a printer, modem, terminal, or other peripheral unit. ASCII (American Standard Code for Information Interchange) codes permit the computer to communicate with other devices. When a keyboard character is typed, it is converted into an ASCII code number and sent to the printer which in turn interprets it as a command. The basic ASCII character code set contains 96 letters, numbers, and symbols; the full ASCII set consists of 128 characters including special symbols and control codes.

Figure A.5   ASCII Code Samples

ASCII Code	Character
032	(space)
038	&
047	/
057	9
065	A
098	b

7

ASCII code conversion
A utility file or program accompanying some WPs designed to change a standard ASCII file to a text file compatible with the particular WP. Since not all text files created by different WPs are compatible or interchangeable, the ASCII code conversion program is necessary if a file is to work with another program. Samna Word III, for instance, has a "translate utility" to perform this type of operation as well as to reverse the process, i.e., convert its files to the ASCII code.

ASCII file
A collection of related records using the American Standard Code for Information Interchange. There are two kinds of ASCII files for computer users, the line-oriented, which requires a carriage return following each line; and the paragraph-oriented, in which a marker is placed at the end of each paragraph. ASCII files can be read by other programs.

ASCII keyboard
A keyboard with keys for all ASCII character sets.

Assembly language
Machine language converted into mnemonic codes. Machine language, with its infinite variety of digits, is more difficult for the programmer to remember than the more user-friendly mnemonic codes of three letters. Assembly language transmits instructions to the computer by using English-like abbreviations and words, such as JMP for jump and LDA for load the accumulator. Each microprocessor uses a different assembly language. See also Machine language, Mnemonic command.

Assignable function key
One of the 10 function keys of the IBM computer and any of its compatibles, to which a

multistroke command is assigned. By using the single-stroke function keys, WPs such as Word-Star can save the user many unnecessary keystrokes and much time in entering special commands such as "set left margin," "set help level," etc. See also Function key.

Attribute
A command that directs the printer to perform a particular print function such as boldface, double-wide print, italics, subscripts, superscripts, and underlining. WPs usually allow attributes to be entered before or after text is typed. If attributes are entered before, such as in preparation for a block of text to be printed in italics, these commands are called automatic attributes. Some users type text and add attributes later to the desired word or blocks of words. See also Command, Dot command, Embedded command.

Figure A.6   Attributes for Easywriter II
With Juki 6300 Printer

Attribute	Print Function
<Alternate>B	Boldface ON
<Alternate>S	Shadow Print ON
<Alternate>U	Superscript ON
<Alternate>D	Subscript ON
<Alternate>N	Normal (above OFF)
<Alternate>_	Underline

Automatic attribute. See Attribute.

Automatic backup
A feature of some WPs which periodically saves
the current text file as it is being worked
on. The automatic backup may be accomplished
in various ways, depending on the particular
program. The Final Word, for instance, calls
this function "state save." It monitors the
keyboard, waiting for a seven-second pause, at
which time it saves the entire document onto a
disk. See also Backup.

Automatic centering. See Centering a line,
    Centering text.

Automatic hyphenation. See Hyphenation.

Automatic line spacing. See Line spacing.

Automatic pagination
A function of almost all WPs. The user can
start numbering the pages to be printed with
almost any digit. The WP handles the rest by
automatically increasing the number in increments of one on each successive page and in
any predetermined position. More sophisticated
WPs provide alternate page numbers. See also
Alternate page numbers.

Automatic paragraph reform
A feature that reconstructs an edited paragraph so that it conforms to pre-set or predetermined parameters. For example, with Word-
Star, the user must press Control B after a
paragraph has been edited so that it can be
reformed. On other WPs, such as WordStar 2000
or Applewriter IIe, the paragraph is reformed
automatically. See also Paragraph reformatting.

Automatic save
A feature of a WP which saves text automatically. Some WPs save the document on screen as
a matter of routine just before the user exits

the program. Others save the text if there is
a pause of a few seconds in the use of the
keyboard. MultiMate uses a different procedure: When the cursor is moved to the next
page, the WP saves the page that was being
worked on. See also Save.

Automatic search and replace. See Global
    search and replace.

Automatic underscore. See Autoscore.

Automatic update
A feature which automatically saves text as it
is entered or revised. Samna Word III, for
example, offers this function, storing text
revisions on disk almost immediately. This can
be a valuable feature, especially during power
failures in which conventional WPs tend to
lose all documents in memory. With automatic
update, only the last three or four lines will
be lost. See also Save.

Autoscore
A feature used to underline text automatically. Also known as automatic underscore. See
also Underlining.

Auxiliary storage
A method of storing data that supplements the
main storage of a computer system. For example, magnetic disk and tape are common auxiliary storage media.

Available memory
An item on the status display or status line
of many WPs which informs the user of the
amount of memory available for writing a file
or document. For instance, if the available
memory feature lists "72% Free," this indicates that 28 percent of the editor's memory
has been consumed. See also RAM, Status display.

B

Background mode
A function provided by certain WPs which allows the user to edit a document while the printer is printing another. Many programs allow only one task at a time to be performed, e.g., editing or printing. Those with the background mode feature offer greater flexibility. By placing the program in background mode, the text enters a "spooler" (simultaneous peripheral operation on-line) which handles the "background" document to be printed. Meanwhile, the computer displays the "foreground" document, ready for editing. WP programs such as MultiMate provide background and foreground print modes. See also Print spooler.

Backing up files. See Backup.

Backspace key
A key used to move the cursor to the left one character at a time, replacing each character with a blank space. Its general function is to delete text that has just been typed. The backspace key is often described as "destructive" because it permanently erases text characters. However, on some WPs there is a "non-destructive" backspace key, which merely moves

the cursor left without altering any of the characters. WordStar is one program with a nondestructive key.

Figure B.1   Example of Backspace

```
        (_ = cursor position)

          (before backspace)

Halley's Comet will be visible to the
naked eye in the southern United States
in January 1986. _

     (after destructive backspace)

Halley's Comet will be visible to the
naked eye in the southern United States _

     (after nondestructive backspace)

Halley's Comet will be visible to the
naked eye in the southern United States
in January 1986.
```

Backspace strikeover. See Overstrike.

Backup
To make a duplicate copy of a file or a disk.
Disks can wear out, be misplaced, or get
damaged; therefore, copies should be made and
the originals stored in a safe place. Duplicates can easily be made from the system's
copy programs or from commercial copy programs. Some professionals recommend having
more than one copy available and devising a
schedule that rotates these copies. See also
Automatic backup.

Backward search
A feature of many WPs which can locate words or phrases with the cursor at the end of the document. This can be useful during the search or search and replace function. Often the WP program requires that the cursor be returned to the beginning of the text before the search can begin; otherwise, the program will not find the desired text. With the backward search feature, the program operates faster and more efficiently. See also Global search and replace, Search and replace.

BASIC
A programming language that uses English-like commands. An acronym for Beginner's All-purpose Symbolic Instruction Code, BASIC is the easiest language to use. Beginners, especially, find the commands, such as Get, Goto, Run, and End, simple to learn.

Batch processing
In word processing, a series of commands which a computer will read and perform automatically. For instance, if the user will be referring to various files and programs during the word processing session, the files can be batch processed to lead automatically into a RAM drive or a hard disk drive. These programs can include a spelling checker, a keyboard enhancer, the WP program itself, and a print buffer. Batch processing is a time-saving way of loading multiple files.

Baud rate
The measurement at which digital data are transmitted in bits per second, or bps. The rate normally ranges up to 19.2K baud (19,200 baud).

Bidirectional printing
The ability of a printer to print in both directions. In bidirectional printing, the

printer operates from left to right, line
feeds without a carriage return, and continues
to print from right to left. Bidirectional
printing eliminates the time necessary for a
carriage return at the end of a line. See also
Printer.

Binary file
One of the methods employed by a WP to store a
document on disk. Binary files have the advantage of occupying less space than other types
such as text files. Estimates range to a saving of as much as 20 percent in the number of
disk sectors used. Many electronic communications systems, however, are designed for text,
rather than for binary files. To compensate
for this, many WPs provide a utility program
which converts binary files into standard text
files. See also Text file, Utility program.

Binary system
A method of programming using the digits "1"
and "0" which combine either to form numbers
or designate plus or minus, yes or no, or on
or off. For instance, the decimal numbers "5,"
"10," and "15" would appear as the binaries
"101," "1010," and "1111," respectively. WPs
design their files according to different
systems, including binary, text, etc.

Bit
The smallest unit that a computer can distinguish. In the binary system, the bit is a
binary digit, a unit of information which
corresponds to a choice between two alterna-
tives such as yes and no or 1 and 0.

Blank disk
A new disk waiting to be formatted or initialized. A blank disk will not store any data
or information without first being formatted.
Blank disks should conform to the system for
which they are intended, e.g., single-side

double-density, double-side double-density, etc.

Blank out text
A function of some WPs permitting the user to erase text and replace it with blank spaces. Blank out text differs from the delete function, which removes text and pulls characters located to the right of the cursor to fill the blank spaces. Text can usually be blanked out by word, line, sentence, or paragraph.

Block
A body of text, usually targeted to be moved, deleted, or stored on disk for future use. Some WPs, such as WordStar 2000, can manipulate vertical as well as horizontal blocks of text. Vertical, or columnar, blocks of figures can also be sorted and added by various WPs. A block of text must first be marked before any of the above options can be performed. See also Block copy, Block editing, Block move, Vertical block.

Block buffer
A part of the computer memory used to temporarily store characters for eventual block move or block copy. Block buffers are considered volatile and temporary storage methods, since any information contained in them will be lost when the power source is turned off. See also Buffer, Print buffer, Text buffer, Volatile storage.

Block copy
The ability to insert a paragraph or block of text into more than one place in a document or into other files. The size of the block of text depends on the memory of the computer and the amount of remaining space in the file. WPs perform block copy in various ways. A typical approach is to place the cursor at the beginning of the text to be copied and press a

command. The cursor is then moved to the end
of the block followed by another command. The
block is now designated by markers or may
appear in inverse video. The cursor can now be
moved to another location in the document
where the block, which has been stored in a
block buffer, can be duplicated. See also
Block editing, Block move.

Block editing
The ability to move, copy, or delete an entire
segment of text. Some WPs allow the user to
edit an unlimited number of words or lines of
text as long as they are labeled correctly.
This procedure usually entails moving the
cursor to the beginning and to the end of the
block to be edited and "marking" it. With some
programs the text is highlighted or displayed
in inverse video; with others, symbols appear
in the places marked by the cursor. The block
can then be erased, moved elsewhere, copied,
saved, or appended to another document at the
cursor position. See also Block move.

Block menu
A list of options or commands designed to
control blocks of text. A block may refer to a
sentence, one or more paragraphs, or a complete document. The block menu permits the
user to move, remove, store, or delete blocks
of text. See also Block buffer, Block copy.

Block move
The ability to move a paragraph or block of
text from one place in a document to another
or to a different file. Block moves are important in editing documents and save time by
eliminating repeated typing. The function
usually consists of a few steps in which a
paragraph or block of text is "marked" by
special function keys, followed by a command
designating where the block should go. The
number of characters of the block of text

marked for moving depends on the size of the computer memory or the number of kilobytes.

Figure B.2   Example of Block Move

(before)

     Not all computers are compatible with each other. Some systems may look alike, but they cannot exchange data.

 AltBOne way to check whether there is compatibility between systems is to try to boot up a program disk. Another way is to check the manual to see what type of DOS the computer requires.AltB

(after)

     Not all computers are compatible with each other. One way to check whether there is compatibility between systems is to try to boot up a program disk. Another way is to check the computer manual to see what type of DOS the computer requires. Some systems may look alike, but they cannot exchange data.

Boilerplating
The ability to combine the contents of other files with a file currently being edited. For instance, stock paragraphs from form letters or a separate file of paragraphs or blocks of text can be accumulated for use in future letters or documents. With boilerplating, one or more of these passages can be inserted into a document presently on screen.

Figure B.3   Example of Boilerplating

```
                  (boilerplate)

The Oryx Press
2214 North Central
Phoenix, Arizona 85004

   (use of boilerplate in letter A)

The Oryx Press
2214 North Central
Phoenix, Arizona 85004


Dear Mr. Smith:

In answer to your letter of December
15 regarding your book, it has been...

   (use of boilerplate in letter B)

The Oryx Press
2214 North Central
Phoenix, Arizona 85004

Dear Mr. Jones:

Thank you for expressing interest in
our publication.  We have directed...
```

Boldface
A WP option that, when compatible with the
printer, prints text darker than conventional
print for emphasis. Boldface is usually accomplished by programming the printer to type
over the characters a second time. Some WPs
display boldface in inverse video on screen,
while others, such as WordStar, signify boldface by enclosing the text in control charac-

ters. Boldface is sometimes called double
print or bold print by some WP and printer
manufacturers. Not all programs are capable of
producing boldface type. Both dot-matrix and
daisy wheel printers can print boldface. See
also Shadow print.

Figure B.4   Example of Boldface

(as it appears on screen)

Alt-BBoldfaceAlt-B is a useful
feature when it is used for emphasis.

(as it appears in print)

Boldface is a useful feature when
it is used for emphasis.

Boot
To start or restart a computer system or a
program. Booting clears the computer and loads
a program into its main memory. The computer
"reads" instructions from a storage device
such as a program disk and enters the data
into its memory. Some software programs are
bootable, while others require booting from
the Disk Operating System. Computers with both
hard and soft disk drives can be configured to
boot from either drive.

Bottom margin
The space, measured either in inches or line
spaces, from the bottom of a sheet of paper to
the last line of print. Bottom margins can be
set by either the printer or the WP, the
latter usually employing line spaces. Some WPs
provide embedded commands and/or print menus
to control the bottom margin. See also Top
margin.

Bright intensity
The appearance of additional light on portions
of the display screen so that these parts
stand out or are highlighted in contrast to
text or graphics shown in normal intensity.
Some WPs utilize these two intensities simultaneously, such as in menus which highlight
headings as opposed to subheadings. Often the
text itself is in bright intensity, while
menus appear in normal intensity. The brightness and contrast controls of the monitor may
have to be adjusted on some systems to distinguish between bright and normal intensity when
this feature is implemented. See also Highlighting.

Buffer
An area located in the computer's memory designed to store information related to a WP. A
buffer is often divided into sections, each
serving a separate function. For example, a
document may occupy one segment, while the WP
program itself rests in another. AppleWriter
II reserves another section of the buffer for
additional subdivisions. These include, among
others, individual buffers for each of the
following: a character deletion, word and
paragraph deletion, print value, glossary, and
footnote buffer. A buffer may also serve as a
storage facility for moving data between devices that work at different speeds. See also
Block buffer, Print buffer, Text buffer.

Bug
An error in the logic of a software program.
Bugs can cause the program to repeat itself,
freeze, or display odd characters on the
screen, all of which interfere with the smooth
operation of the software. Correcting these
anomalies is known as debugging the program.

21

Bullet
A text formatting or layout technique in which
each indented item begins with a "o," a dot,
or some other character in the left margin
with successive items similarly indented.

Figure B.5   Example of Bullets

Bullets can serve many functions:

• They help to emphasize the text on the
  written page

• They offer another method of outlining,
  although not as formal as the conventional outline

• They help to break up large blocks of
  print that are difficult to read

Bundled software
A package of programs usually included with
the purchase of a computer. Bundled software
often contains a WP, a database program, and a
spreadsheet. These programs, although presented gratis by the computer manufacturer,
are not necessarily inferior to other software
in related categories. In fact, the packages
often include well-known brands of WPs, such
as WordStar or Perfect Writer. Sometimes
bundled software is a temporary, special offer, designed to boost sluggish sales of the
hardware; in other cases it is a permanent
part of the complete package.

Byte
A term indicating a portion of consecutive
binary digits, or group of bits, such as an 8-
bit or 16-bit byte. Also, computer language

for one character. Also, a standard for measuring memory, such as a computer with 64K of memory (64,000 bytes) or a disk capacity of 360K.

C

Call symbol
In relation to footnoting, the character used
to enumerate the reference. Call symbols can
be numbers, letters, or other characters such
as asterisks. Some WPs such as WordPerfect
offer all three of the above as style choices,
while other programs limit the call symbol to
numbers.

Caps lock key
The keyboard function that controls the case
of the letter keys. The caps lock key operates
in the same manner as a toggle switch: When
it is pressed once, any letters that are typed
will appear in upper case; when it is pressed
a second time, all the letters will show up in
lower case. The caps lock key, unlike the
shift key, does not affect the keyboard symbols. On some computer systems, the key has a
built-in red indicator lamp which lights up to
remind the user that it is on. See also Keyboard, Shift key, Toggle.

Card
A peripheral device usually installed into a
slot inside the computer. This internal accessory can connect a modem to the system, add
another disk drive, increase the current RAM

of the computer, etc. Also called peripheral cards, these devices are limited to the number of slots or sockets available in the individual machine, which may vary from none to eight. See also Modem, Peripheral, RAM.

Caret
A nonprinting character used in some WPs which is embedded in documents to denote the beginning or end of a particular printing technique. Carets are often used to embed commands for underlining, boldface, subscripts, and superscripts. The caret is also used as a symbol on screen for the control key in WPs such as WordStar. See also Embedded command.

Figure C.1   Caret as Nonprinting Character

(as it appears on screen)

Embedded commands help WPs produce functions such as superscripts (86^So^S) and subscripts (H^U2^U0).

(as it appears in print)

Embedded commands help WPs produce functions such as superscripts (86°) and subscripts (H_2O).

Figure C.2   Caret as Symbol

^S character left	^D character right
^A word left	^F word right
^G left margin	^H right margin

Carriage return

A function borrowed from typing and now applied to computers. The enter or return key performs the carriage return task by ending one paragraph and preparing to begin another. When typing past the end of a line on a computer display screen, the text "word wraps" around to the next line, all the information being treated as one paragraph. If the enter or return key is pressed when the end of the line is reach, the cursor, like a carriage return on a conventional typewriter, moves to the next line. Some WPs mark each carriage return with a nonprintable symbol in the right margin.

Figure C.3 Example of Carriage Return Symbol

Some WPs mark the end of a paragraph with a carriage return symbol such as a "smaller than" sign. <

Case

A term used to define capital and small letters. Upper-case refers to capital letters and lower-case refers to small letters. Some early computers, such as the Apple II, were capable of typing only upper-case letters, which made these models ineffectual as word processing machines.

Case-sensitive function

A feature which searches and replaces text by either upper or lower case. Most WPs do not differentiate between upper- and lower-case letters during the search mode. However, during the replace mode, whatever case is entered will occur on screen. With the case-sensitive function activated, the user can locate only the characters that match the string designated. This feature distinguishes between upper- and lower-case characters.

Catalog
A list of file names representing documents stored on one data disk. Also, a list of programs on a system or program disk. Some computers, such as the Apple and similar models, use the term "catalog," while others, like the IBM and compatible systems, refer to this listing of files as a directory. Appearing next to the name of each file can be found the number of sectors or the number of bytes of each file, the type of file (text, etc.), and the latest date of entry. Many WPs such as the now defunct AceWriter make a distinction between program and data disks in the type of information supplied with each. Notice in the first example below that formatted (F) and unformatted (U) text files are differentiated preceding the number indicating sectors used. The second example is a listing of all files on the disk including binary (B) and text (T), which was brought to the screen by typing "CATALOG." See also Directory.

Figure C.4   A Sample Catalog
of the Acewriter Data Disk

```
F009 REPORT1
F032 REPORT2
U017 LETTER1
U006 LETTER2
```

Figure C.5   Acewriter's Complete
File Listing

```
B 021 LABELS
B 033 PRINTER
T 009 REPORT1
T 032 REPORT2
```

Center justification

The placement of text in the center of a page through the use of certain WP commands. A line or an entire document can be center justified, depending on the parameters set by the user. Some WPs do not supply the center justification feature, but offer only a right justify option. Other programs provide a format file with three options: left justify, center justify, full justify (with left and right margins). Centering a line, which is the same as center justify but on a smaller scale, appears on many more WPs than does center justify.

Figure C.6   Example of
Center Justification

Center justification
is a handy feature,
especially for designing the following:
signs
posters
titles of works

Centering a line

A feature of many WPs which allows a line of text such as a title or subheading to be centered automatically. Centering a line with these programs is usually a simple procedure, requiring little more than finding the proper submenu, followed by pressing a character such as "C." With some WPs the user may also center a line by typing in an embedded command which is displayed on screen but does not appear in print. Applewriter II, for instance, performs this function with a dot command (.cj) before the line to be centered and a command (.lj) following the line to continue with left justified text in the remainder of the document. Dot commands sometimes are faster to apply, since the user does not have to leave the text mode for other menus. But they disrupt the screen format, making it difficult to judge how the text will look in print.

Figure C.7   Centering a Line
with AppleWriter II

```
          (as it appears on screen)

.cj
Today's Menu
.lj

          (as it appears in print)

              Today's Menu
```

Centering text
To format text so that it appears in the middle of the page with ragged left and right margins. See also Center justification, Centering a line.

Central processing unit. See CPU.

Chaining. See File chaining.

Change logged disk drive
A function on the opening menu of WordStar that refers to the default drive or the drive in use. Changing the drive allows the user to transfer files from one disk to another. This frees space on the disk in the default drive. See also Default drive, Logged disk.

Changing fonts. See Font.

Character
Any number, letter, or symbol. A character

occupies one space or column in relation to WP programs. Characters can either emanate from a keyboard or be created by the computer user and are printable either on screen or by the printer. Control characters and embedded commands are exceptions; these appear on the screen but not on the printed page. With WP programs that feature microjustification, characters that appear on the page occupying less than one space still take one column on the display screen.

Character sequence
An arrangement of characters designed so that they form an embedded command. This type of character sequence is displayed on screen but does not appear on the printed page. The period often precedes such a sequence, as in .RM60, which sets the right margin at the sixtieth column. This is often called a dot command. Periods are used to specify dot commands, since normal text virtually never starts with this character.

Character set
The letters and numbers the driver program of a WP produces on screen. Some character sets are more legible than others. This can mean less eyestrain after long sessions in front of the computer terminal. Some character sets are more ornate than others, adding serifs to their letters, etc.

Character string
A sequence of characters including letters, numbers, punctuation marks, spaces, etc. A word is an example of a character string. Character strings are important during the search and replace function. For instance, to find the word "and," the program directs the computer to search for all cases of "and." This includes not only the separate word, but

instances in which "and" is part of other words such as "standing." With many WPs, the entity "and" can be found alone by placing a space before and after the word. The standard search and replace procedure requires entering the string to be found and, at the replace prompt, entering the string which will replace the original. Also known as string, text string. See also Search and replace.

Characters per inch. See Cpi.

Characters per second. See Cps.

CHKDSK
A command for finding out the amount of space available on a disk and whether all files have been properly recorded. When this message is typed, a WP utility program analyzes the directory and file of a specific drive and provides a memory status report on the screen. With WPs that do not have this feature, CHKDSK can be entered through the disk operating system. When this command is typed at the prompt and Enter is pressed, the screen will display the following: the number of bytes used, the number of disk files, and the number of bytes available on disk.

Clear
A function that permits a file in memory to be deleted. Because of the potential loss of valuable data, the WP usually contains a warning before this function is activated, reminding the user to save the document. The clear function is different from Remove, a term used on some WPs such as PFS: Write. Clear erases only that material in the memory of the computer and what is printed on the screen, not on the disk. Remove permanently deletes files from a disk. It is therefore very important to distinguish between these two functions. See also Remove.

Close up
A method of removing extra spaces in the text.
The typical procedure used to activate this
function is to place the cursor at the beginning of the group of unwanted spaces that are
to be deleted and press the designated function key (backspace, delete, etc.). The blank
spaces will be removed and the next non-blank
character will be placed in the cursor position. This is a simple and useful technique
for deleting unnecessary spaces at the beginning of lines, etc.

Figure C.8   Example of Close Up

```
                    (before)

    Unwanted spaces can easily be re-
moved by placing the cursor _ in _
front of _   them and pressing the¯
proper _¯   function key.

                    (after)

    Unwanted spaces can easily be re-
moved by placing the cursor in front
of them and pressing the proper function
key.
```

Cold start
The process of turning a computer on from the
off position, using DOS, then booting a software program such as a WP. See also Boot.

Color graphics card
An accessory installed internally in a computer slot and designed to operate with a color
monitor. Many owners purchase this card with
the original equipment, including a monochrome
terminal, with intentions of adding a color

display at a later time. Some WPs require a special configuration when using a color graphics card with a monochrome monitor. Otherwise the display screen will appear distorted, especially in terms of its contrast and brightness.

Color monitor
A computer display device which produces a variety of colors by using three electron guns, one for each of the primary colors (red, green, and blue). There are two types of color monitors. The composite video monitor, which resembles the standard color television set, uses one composite signal to control all three electron guns. The RGB (red, green, blue) monitor utilizes a separate signal for each gun. Because of its additional sophistication, the RGB system produces better resolution or sharpness and is preferred over the composite monitor for WPs using an 80-column display. See also Monitor.

Column
A vertical section of a printed page. A column may consist of text, a table of figures, or a combination of both. A column is generally independent of other data on the same page. Some WPs permit columns of text or figures to be moved, saved, or deleted.

Column insert
The ability of a WP to enter a column between current columns. Although this function can be performed manually line by line, a tedious task at best, some WPs produce this effect by extending the format line and adding the spaces automatically. Other programs such as MultiMate provide column insert automatically by using function keys.

Column mode
The ability of a WP to print text with more

than one column on a page. Some WPs find this a difficult task, while others make no provision for it at all. Yet a few programs can not only handle multiple columns, but can format them complete with justification and true proportional spacing. Column mode is a useful feature, particularly when creating newsletters.

Command
An instruction which directs the computer to perform a particular function. In WP, some commands frequently used are Save, Find, Edit, Replace, Delete, Return to Main Menu, etc. Command orders are usually in the form of words and/or numbers which are typed on a keyboard, addressed to a microphone, positioned on a game paddle, etc.

Command-driven WP
A program that performs different functions by means of various commands entered on the keyboard. Command-driven WPs operate quickly by inputting direct commands. The difficulty, however, lies in the user's ability to learn the numerous commands, especially when no mnemonics are employed. WordStar, for example, uses Control QQB to repeat its reformatting function; it uses Control AQ to search for a word, etc. Without a thorough knowledge of or experience with these commands, the user must either continually refer to a help menu or to the documentation or forgo certain functions. The second generation of WPs introduced an extensive use of menus. Menu-driven programs are simpler to operate and learn, but run at a slower pace. See also Menu-driven WP.

Command line
On some WPs, a line usually located near the top or bottom of the screen designed to send instructions to the program. For instance, the user, by typing a number, letter, or word, can

order the WP to get, edit, save, or delete a file; select a disk drive, etc. A command line is often accompanied by a list of functions.

Figure C.9   A Typical Command Line

```
┌─────────────────────────────────────────────┐
│  ─────────────────────────────────────────   │
│                                               │
│  C-CLEAR   D-DELETE E-EDIT   P-PRINT S-SAVE   │
│  ─────────────────────────────────────────   │
└─────────────────────────────────────────────┘
```

Command mode
A function of some WPs designed to display a list of command options. Some programs offer more than 10 commands on one screen. Sometimes the command mode occupies only a single line running horizontally across the top or bottom of the screen. Some of these permit the user to load a file into the computer memory, to format blank disks, to delete files on disk, etc. Command modes are simple to use, often requiring only one keystroke of a number or letter relating to a specific function.

Figure C.10   A Sample Command Mode Listing

```
┌─────────────────────────────────────────────┐
│           1 - LOAD A FILE                     │
│           2 - EDIT A FILE                     │
│           3 - SAVE A FILE                     │
│           4 - REMOVE A FILE                   │
│           5 - PRINT A FILE                    │
│           6 - COPY A FILE                     │
│           7 - EXIT TO DOS                     │
│                                               │
│           ENTER A NUMBER _                    │
└─────────────────────────────────────────────┘
```

Comment line
A feature of some WPs such as Newscript which

allows the user to enter personal notes within
the text of a document, which then appear on
screen but not on the printed page. These
programs accomplish this through the use of
commands. Comment lines can be helpful re-
minders to the user. They can relate to revisions yet to be made, print formatting, further research, or unrelated topics such as
calling the office or picking up the laundry.

Compass layout
A "diamond-shaped" arrangement of four keys
for the movement of the cursor resembling the
four points of a compass. For example, some
WPs select the keys "I," "J," "K," and "M"
because of their layout on the keyboard. "I"
is to the north and therefore represents the
cursor's movement one line up; "J," to the
west, cursor left one space; etc. Also known
as diamond layout.

Figure C.11   Compass Layout
Using I, J, K, and M

```
            I

        J     K

            M
```

Compatibility
The ability of different components to operate
together. Also, the ability of one computer
system to accept and process information developed by another system without any modification. For instance, there are many IBM-
compatible computers on the market, but not
all of these models are 100 percent-compatible
with the IBM in terms of software. Some programs which run on the PC will not work on

similar machines. In computer hardware, the system must be compatible with the printer; in software, the program should be compatible with the operating system.

Compress
A function of some WPs which removes extraneous spaces after text has been edited. Sometimes multiple spaces appear after a session of editing. The compress feature, which works globally, reduces multiple spaces to one, except at the end of a sentence. In this instance two spaces are left. With some WPs Compress deletes "soft" hyphens when they occur anywhere other than at the end of a line.

Figure C.12   Example of Compress

(before)

The compress   feature removes extra   spaces from a document   after it has been   edited. This   can be an important   time-saving function.

(after)

The compress feature removes extra spaces from a document after it has been edited.   This can be an important time-saving function.

Compressed mode
A method of printing a document in smaller type. Compressed mode usually contains 15 or 17 characters per inch, or cpi, whereas normal mode produces 10 or 12 cpi. Compressed mode is often used to quote passages, to place footnotes at the bottom of a page, or simply to

save space. When this size or pitch, as it is sometimes called, is used with a dot-matrix printer, it usually cannot be printed in enhanced or correspondence-quality mode. See also Dot-matrix printer.

Computer
A machine designed to accept and store instructions and execute them. A computer can also receive and transmit data and process and store different forms of information. See also Microcomputer, Personal computer.

Computer memory
That part of the computer used to store information supplied by a keyboard, a disk, or a modem. Computer memory is volatile, since it can be lost when the power fails or is turned off. That is why it must be saved to disk. Also, computer memory is limited. The amount, measured in kilobytes, depends on the particular computer and additional "memory boards." Memory usually ranges from 64K to 128K with machines such as the Commodore and from 256K to 640K with IBMs and compatibles with a board installed in one of the internal slots of the computer. The larger the computer memory, the more sophisticated the software that can be used and the larger the document it can contain for editing. See also RAM, ROM.

Condensed print. See Compressed mode.

Conditional page break
A command which produces a new page if fewer than a designated number of lines remain. Conditional page breaks override standard page breaks. For example, a page of text may have three or four lines remaining at the bottom, and a chart, table, or new subheading is coming up. The user will probably prefer to start this new material on the next page. By installing a dot command with a number, which in-

forms the program where to end a page, the user can alter the default page break so that the new text prints at the top of a new page. See also Discretionary page break, Page break.

Conditional replacement
An option of some WPs with the search and replace feature. Conditional replacement permits the user to view each occurrence before deciding whether or not to make any change. The search and replace function offers other options as well. See also Global search and replace, Search and replace.

Configuration. See Printer configuration.

Continuous on-screen help. See On-screen help.

Control character
An ASCII character used by many WPs to communicate with a printer, thereby causing it to perform a special function. See also ASCII code, Control code.

Control code
A configuration produced by the keyboard control key plus another character, both of which appear on the screen but do not print out in the hard copy. Control codes are used with many WPs to initiate underlining, boldface, superscripts, subscripts, etc. These codes are usually placed before and after the text and are called start and stop control codes. The use of control codes alone does not necessarily guarantee that a particular function will operate; usually the program must be configured for each individual printer, etc. Some WPs provide a method of subduing the control codes on the screen. Also, control codes appearing on screen do not disturb the right justification of the text, although they do tend to overrun a typed line with programs such as WordStar. Some software programs de-

pict functions such as underlining or boldface on screen in inverse video, thereby eliminating the need for control codes as a means of identification.

Figure C.13   Control Codes

(as they appear on screen)

In Shakespeare's ^VE^VHamlet^VR^V...

(as they appear on printed page)

In Shakespeare's Hamlet...

Control key
A key always used in conjunction with another key to perform a particular task or command. For example, with some WPs, Control L will load a file into memory; Control P will print a file; Control B will move the cursor to the beginning of a document, etc. When the control key plus another character is pressed on the keyboard, these commands do not appear in the final printout, although they may be displayed in the text on the screen.

Control sequence
The use by a WP of a series of keystrokes, usually beginning with the control key. Some control sequences can prove to be rather unwieldy, especially when they make no mnemonic references to the function they are performing. WordStar, for instance, uses Control QQB to repeat the reformatting of each paragraph in edited text. Also, Control KD ends the editing process, saves the text to disk, and returns the program to the opening menu.

Converting text files

A utility program supplied by some WPs which permits changing the files created with that particular program so that they can be loaded into and edited by another WP. Programs such as The Write Choice and Bank Street Writer, for instance, provide a utility that converts their binary files into text files so that they can be read by Screenwriter II and other WPs.

Copy

To duplicate text, parts of text, documents, disks, etc. Reasons the user might wish to copy text include: to have a backup copy, to edit a copy while preserving the original, or to add the text eventually to another file or document. Copies can be produced in various ways. Almost all WPs permit the user to copy text or a portion of it. This may be stored in a buffer or saved on disk. To prevent the new information from overwriting the file already on disk, the user should give the document a different file name. A text file may also be copied using DOS commands. Again, the file should be given a different name so that it does not write over the same file on the disk. Documents on screen are usually copied by way of a menu command or option. Parts of text often require control key commands or embedded commands. Complete disks are copied only through DOS. WPs offer a variety of copy pro- cedures, including Copy to Disk, Copy to Printer, Copy to Buffer, and Copy to Screen.

Copy buffer. See Text buffer.

Copy-protected

A code placed on software to prevent dupli- cates from being made. Copy-protected programs such as WPs cannot be stored on hard disks. Although vendors use this technique to prevent unauthorized copies from being made, which

might result in lost sales, it provides certain inconveniences for the purchaser who
cannot make backup copies. Some companies,
however, do offer a copy for an additional fee
or allow a few archival duplicates to be made
from the original.

Copy text. <u>See</u> Duplicate text.

Correspondence quality
The highest-quality print mode of a dot-matrix
printer. Dot-matrix printers frequently support three modes of printing. Draft quality is
the fastest, but creates the lightest print;
the dots that make up the characters are most
noticeable. Double-strike or enhanced mode
produces darker print but doesn't operate as
fast as draft mode. Correspondence quality,
which sometimes approaches letter quality or
the quality of text produced by a typewriter,
prints at the slowest speed to achieve its
high quality. To produce correspondence quality, the print head prints each character
twice, the second time hitting the ribbon
slightly off center. This second strike fills
in much of the spacing between the dots which
form the characters.

Cpi
Characters per inch, or the number of letters,
symbols, or numbers which fit into a one-inch
horizontal line. Many printers provide a range
of cpi, for example, from 10 to 15 or 17 cpi.
WPs can control cpi or print density from four
to 24 cpi, depending on the capabilities of
the individual printer. The default value of
most WPs and printers is 10 cpi.

CP/M
Control Program for Microcomputers. CP/M, in
various formats, is a very popular operating
system for which many software programs have
been written. CP/M programs can be run on a

wide range of computers, including Apple
machines, which require the installation of a
special board. Computers that use this operating system allow their users to select from
thousands of programs in every field from
games to esoteric professions.

Cps

Characters per second, or the number of characters produced by a printer in one second.
Usually, dot-matrix printers can print more
cps than daisy wheel machines. Many of these
impact printers can reach speeds of 160 to 180
cps in data processing mode. Some advanced
models achieve speeds of well over 200 cps.
However, for correspondence or near-letter
quality, the speed is often drastically re-
duced to about 40 cps. Daisy wheel printers
usually offer only one speed, with the low-end
models printing at 18 to 20 cps, the mid-range
printers at approximately 35 cps, and the top-
of-the-line models at about 55 cps. With these
printers, the speed of the machine does not
affect the quality of the output. See also
Daisy wheel printer, Dot-matrix printer.

CPU

The central processing unit, or "brain," of a
computer. The CPU executes all computer operations, such as arithmetic functions. Every
computer has three essential parts: a CPU, a
memory system, and a method of getting data
into and out of the computer.

Crash

The failure of a program to continue to operate or to extricate itself from a problem. A
WP that crashes usually freezes on screen.
Eventually, when the program is rebooted, any
documents in memory are lost forever. Some WPs
are more susceptible to power surges or fluc-
tuations in power lines than others. These
problems can also lead to crashing. This is

less disastrous in programs that provide automatic update, a feature which continually stores documents in memory onto a data disk. See also Automatic update.

Crash recovery
The ability of a WP program to extricate itself from a problem without losing the document on screen. When a program crashes, it may result in a locked file or a "frozen" screen in which text cannot be edited, the cursor cannot be moved, and commands such as Save and Print cannot be activated. In many cases exiting from the program results in the loss of the current data. Some WPs provide crash recovery, which allows editing to continue and restores the use of the cursor. This can sometimes be accomplished simply by pressing Escape. Other means may require a more complex series of commands to be entered. WPs with automatic backup offer some relief, since most of the document has been saved to disk as a regular routine.

CRT
Cathode ray tube. The CRT is the picture tube or the face of the monitor or video display. The CRT comes in monochrome or in color. The monochrome models display a green or an amber image. See also Color monitor, Monitor.

Cursor
A symbol which denotes where the next character will appear on screen. A cursor may be a small vertical rectangle, a blinking rectangle, a small horizontal bar, a double bar, etc. Some WP programs utilize one cursor symbol for the edit mode and another for overwrite. The more flexible the cursor, the more efficient the WP program. For example, some programs can move the cursor to the beginning and end of text, jump the cursor to the end of a word, line or paragraph, etc. Virtually all

WPs use a cursor symbol. The cursor is sometimes called a cursor character.

Cursor character. <u>See</u> Cursor.

Cursor control
A WP's capability to guide the cursor to any
part of the screen. A WP program may utilize
the cursor control keys of the computer keyboard or, in lieu of these, manipulate the
cursor by means of a combination of the control or alternate keys with others. Some of
the more popular cursor controls include moving the cursor to the left or right; by a
character, word, or line at a time; or up and
down by page, screen, or entire document. The
more choices of cursor movement a WP offers,
the easier and quicker it becomes to edit a
document.

Cursor-control diamond. <u>See</u> Compass layout.

Cursor control key
A key used to manipulate the cursor up, down,
left, or right. The basic cursor control keys
are the four arrow keys to the right of the
alphanumeric or conventional typewriter keyboard. They are usually placed in a "diamond"
or "compass" layout so that the position of
each resembles the function of the key, e.g.,
the left arrow key (<--), which moves the
cursor one space to the left, is located on
the left side of the diamond. Some of the
Apple computers, however, place these cursor
control keys in a horizontal line at the bottom of the keyboard. <u>See</u> <u>also</u> Arrow key,
Compass layout.

Cursor movement
The navigation of the cursor around the text
and the display screen. WPs provide such
varied movement as bringing the cursor to the
next character, word, line, sentence, or para-

graph; top or bottom of the screen or document; previous page or screen, etc. Cursor
movements occur by the use of control keys,
arrow keys, special function keys, combinations of shift and alternate keys, etc.

Figure C.14   Sample Cursor Movement Chart

Cursor Left One Character	Left Arrow
Cursor Right One Character	Right Arrow
Cursor Up One Line	Up Arrow
Cursor Down One Line	Down Arrow
Cursor to Top of File	Home Key
Cursor to End of File	End Key

Cursor quantity key
An arrow or other designated key designed or
assigned to move the cursor a number of spaces
such as a word, line, sentence, or paragraph
at a time. Cursor quantity keys often work in
conjunction with other keys. Samna Word III,
for example, pairs up these keys with the
delete key to erase the amount of text designated by the quantity key.

Custom dictionary
A series of entries added as a separate file
to a spelling checker. These checkers usually
contain a main dictionary, consisting of from
20,000 to approximately 80,000 words and a
supplemental dictionary of less commonly used
words, including entries with prefixes, suffixes, and plurals. The custom dictionary is
user-initiated, often composed of names,
titles, and terms frequently used in a partic-

ular document or report. For example, if a
scientific paper is to be written on a WP, it
would be expedient to create a custom dictionary of scientific terms likely to be used
often in this text but not found in the main
dictionary. When the document is completed, it
can be checked for spelling by this custom
dictionary as well as the main one. Many spelling checkers permit the construction of a
custom dictionary. See also Dictionary, Supplemental dictionary.

Custom font. See Font.

Cut and paste. See Document assembly.

D

Daisy wheel printer
A printing device which uses a flat element
consisting of "petals" with characters. This
element, called a daisy wheel, spins while a
"hammer" hits each particular character. Daisy
wheel printers produce letter-quality printing, as opposed to dot-matrix printers, which
provide correspondence-quality text. Although
they offer higher-quality print than dot-
matrix printers and interchangeable fonts,
daisy wheel printers are generally slower. See
also Dot-matrix printer.

Darkness degree
The amount of emphasis or darkness that can be
accomplished with boldface during the printout. Some WPs such as Newscript allow the user
to control the degree of darkness employed to
the double print or boldface feature. This
function depends on the ability of the printer
to handle such a command. See also Boldface,
Shadow print.

Data
Encoded information entered or extracted from
a computer. The term "data" is sometimes used
interchangeably with "text," although purists
reserve the former for information involving

spreadsheets and database programs and con-
sider text exclusively the domain of word
processing. To be saved, data must be stored
on a permanent substance, such as tape or
disk, or it will be lost when the computer is
turned off. See also Document, Information,
Text.

Data compression
The ability to store more characters in a
given space than its memory size may indicate.
For instance, some printer buffers offer,
among other advanced features, data compression, which can almost double the amount of
memory. A table or chart normally occupying
about 15K bytes can be compressed into approximately 8K bytes by using an accessory buffer.

Data disk
The plastic storage medium on which documents
on screen are saved and stored as files. Virtually all WPs distinguish between program or
master disks, which contain the WP program
itself, and those that hold text files created
by the WP. Some WPs automatically save and
store text information onto the second disk
drive, which contains the data disk; with
other programs, the data disk drive must be
stipulated. Data disks, also known as destination disks, must first be initialized or formatted before files are stored on them. Formatting can sometimes be done from within a WP
program. If not, the disk can be formatted
through DOS commands. See also Program disk.

Data processing
Changing raw data or information into a usable
format through the use of a computer.

Data processing mode. See Draft mode.

Database
A program that organizes, stores, retrieves,

49

and modifies data and information in lists. The data can be rearranged and sorted alphabetically or numerically. Some databases are part of integrated software that includes a WP and a spreadsheet. In these cases the database file can be loaded into the WP program for editing, visual presentation, and eventual printing. However, there are other database programs that can be incorporated into standalone WPs, whether from the same vendor (PFS: Write and PFS: File) or from separate manufacturers.

Figure D.1   Sample Database Format

SALESMAN:	DATE:
PRODUCT LINE:	TERRITORY:
TOTAL SALES 1986:	1985:
RANK IN SALES 1986:	1985:
NUMBER OF NEW CUSTOMERS:	

Decimal tab
A WP feature designed to align decimal points. The decimal tab is useful in creating charts or typing statistics.

Dedicated function key
A key that performs a unique task. Page up and down, home, end, and the 10 function keys of the IBM and similar keyboards are some of the keys considered dedicated function keys. The Series II Apple computers do not have many of these dedicated keys. See also Function key.

Dedicated WP
A computer designed to perform virtually one

function: word processing. Dedicated WPs, such
as those made by Wang, usually assign specific
function keys to handle particular tasks, such
as search and replace, etc. Conventional personal computers require WP software which
often utilizes several keystrokes to perform
the same function, although these machines can
also run other types of software such as database and spreadsheet programs. This software
is often tailored to imitate the wide range of
features of the dedicated machine. By designing their internal components strictly for WP
functions, dedicated WPs usually offer a higher level of performance than that of personal
computers operating in conjunction with WP
programs. However, some of these programs,
through countless revisions, have evolved to
the point of rivaling the dedicated processor
in the number and sophistication of their WP
features.

Default
A value assigned by a WP or printer when no
other value is supplied. For instance, WPs
usually provide default values for such functions as left and right margins, line spacing,
paper length, etc. Defaults can be changed by
specifying other values. See also Default
value.

Default drive
The disk drive in use during the editing process. Some WPs allow the drive to be changed
from within the program. WordStar, for instance, which calls its default drive its
logged disk, permits the user to change the
drive by way of a menu command. Applewriter II
permits the same function by responding to the
save and load prompts with D1 or D2 following
the file name. Other WPs such as PFS: Write
automatically save files on the second disk
drive once the program is formatted or installed with the particular drive data.

Default page break. See Page break.

Default parameter
A measurement, restriction, or function preset within a WP. Default parameters can control margins, page lengths, justification,
etc. A simple but popular function such as
right justification is handled differently by
different WPs. Most have the default set for
no right justification, while WordStar's default provides right alignment which can be
canceled manually. Almost all WPs allow for
default parameters that affect printing.
These, too, can be changed by the user. Other
programs such as EasyWriter II and The Final
Word permit defaults to be changed by way of
menu-driven utility programs.

Default printer
The printer that a particular WP is designed
to use. Default printer values can be altered
to make them compatible with other printer
models.

Default value
A reply to a menu request as well as other
prompts which have been predetermined by the
software program. Default values selected by
WP programs often are the more commonly used
ones. For example, page length is set at 66
(for 8 1/2 X 11 sheets), number of lines per
page at 55-58, right margin at 65, etc. Default values can also refer to the previous
configurations. In a two-disk-drive system, if
Drive 2 was the last drive in operation, it
may not be necessary to list the drive number
when next saving or loading a document. Default values can be changed to suit the user's
needs. See also Default.

Figure D.2   Example of Default Values
for Printing

```
LEFT MARGIN          9
PARAGRAPH MARGIN     O
RIGHT MARGIN        75
TOP MARGIN           1
BOTTOM MARGIN        1
PAGE NUMBER          1
LINE SPACING         1
PRINTED LINES       55
PAGE LENGTH         66
```

Define block of text
To mark a block of text for moving, copying,
or removing. Blocks of text must be defined or
marked before they can be edited. Some WPs use
characters or symbols to signify which text is
to be moved, etc. Other programs such as PFS:
Write use inverse video to designate the
block. See also Block copy, Block editing,
Block move.

Figure D.3   Defining a Block of Text

```
        ^BM This is the way a block of text
may appear on the screen after it has
been marked for copying, moving, or
removing.^BM
```

Definition
A term used in relation to a WP glossary
referring to the character string or expres-
sion that is represented by the glossary term
or designator. For instance, the term or abbreviation "n" could represent "name," "a"
could stand for "address," and so on. Glossaries simplify entering often-repeated text

such as names, titles, etc. See also Designator, Glossary.

Delete
To remove or erase permanently. Text, parts of
text, even complete documents and files can be
deleted. Deletions can be accomplished in
several ways. With many WPs the delete key may
be used, as can the backspace key. Another
approach is the delete command. Some WPs provide methods of restoring deleted material or
undoing delete commands. In insert mode the
use of the delete function causes text to move
left, replacing the text which was removed. In
overstrike mode, blank spaces replace the
erased text.

Figure D.4   Examples of Delete

```
            (before delete)

     This is an example example of the
delete function in use. It is helpful
in removing unwanted material.

  (after delete in the insert mode)

     This is an example of the delete
function in use. It is helpful in re-
moving unwanted material.

  (after delete in the overstrike mode)

     This is an example          of the
delete function in use. It is helpful
in removing unwanted material.
```

Delete sentence
A command that erases all text starting at the
cursor and ending at the next period. There

are many delete commands, including character, word, line, and block deletion. Some users prefer the delete sentence over the delete line command, since it is more natural to remove a complete thought than it is to eliminate a group of words. See also Delete.

Delimiter
A symbol or character which is used to mark a segment of text a user may wish to save, load, or find. Delimiters may be any character not used in the current WP document. Some WPs restrict the delimiter to particular symbols such as the caret (^) or the backslash (\). See also Marker.

Descender
That part of a lower-case character that extends below the line of other characters. These letters include "g," "j," "p," "q," and "y." Some earlier dot-matrix printers were unable to print descenders and were forced to move these characters up to the base line. Today virtually all types of printing devices (dot matrix, daisy wheel, thermal, and laser) support descenders.

Designator
A keyboard character which represents a text string, especially in terms of a glossary. Designators save time because the user does not have to retype words or phrases, sometimes referred to as definitions, that are used repeatedly. By carefully building a glossary (if the WP has this facility), the user can define "McGuinness" with the designator "M" and "proportional spacing" with "p." Each time one of these designators is typed, the full definition is entered into the document. See also Definition, Glossary.

Destination disk. See Data disk.

Destination drive
The drive containing the disk which will accept a text file or which will hold a copy of
a file or program. With Apple computer systems
the drive is usually referred to as Drive 2;
with IBM and compatible systems the drive is
known as Drive B (or C, if it is the hard disk
drive). The destination drive is sometimes
called the data disk drive.

Destructive backspace
A key which, when pressed, deletes the character to the left of the cursor. The left-arrow
key, which is normally used to return the
cursor to previously entered text, can sometimes erase the characters the cursor moves
over. NewWord is one such program with a destructive backspace. See also Backspace, Non-
destructive backspace.

Destructive insert mode. See Insert.

Diamond layout. See Compass layout.

Dictionary
A utility program often accompanying a WP
which checks documents for spelling errors.
Dictionaries on disk may range from 20,000 to
80,000 words. Smaller dictionaries, besides
containing fewer entries, usually omit prefixes and suffixes such as "pre," "un," and
"ing." Larger dictionaries take longer to
search through the document for errors. Dictionaries may be purchased as accessories to
WPs; they are sold by WP vendors or by independent software publishers. See also Custom
dictionary, Spelling checker, Supplementary
dictionary.

Direct print. See Typewriter mode.

Directory
A list of all the document files stored on

disk. Also, a term used by DOS for a list of all files contained on a disk, including data concerning the file, such as size, date last revised, etc. DOS begins with a main or root directory which specifies files and other directories called subdirectories. In the following example, the directory provides the name of the file, file type, length in bytes, and date and time the file was entered. <u>See also</u> Catalog.

Figure D.5   Sample Directory

COMMAND	COM	17792	10-21-85	11:00p
FORMAT	COM	6912	10-22-85	9:14a
LETTR1	DOC	251	3-19-86	3:43p
LETTR2	DOC	217	3-21-86	4:56p
ANSI	SYS	1449	4-12-86	9:13a
PRNT	BAT	45	4-12-86	10:37a

Discretionary global replace
A subfeature of the search and replace function. In general, Search and Replace allows the user to find a character string and replace it with a corrected or alternate one. Global Search and Replace performs this function automatically through an entire document for every occurrence the program finds. Discretionary Global Replace searches the document, stops at each occurrence, and offers the user the choice of replacing each. <u>See also</u> Global search and replace, Search and replace.

Discretionary page break
A function that allows the user to select any point in a document at which to end a page. Some WPs contain a default page break, a number of lines after which a new page will begin. Sometimes it may be advisable to change this default value so that text, such as a new

chapter, or a chart or graph, starts on the next page. A discretionary page break can be executed by using an embedded dot command in some WPs such as WordStar. See also Conditional page break, Page break.

Disk
A storage medium for information made of thin, plastic material with a magnetic coating. Disks, which can by "floppy" or hard, come in various sizes, including 3 1/2 inches, 5 1/4 inches, and 8 inches. The most popular, especially for home use, is the 5 1/4-inch floppy disk. Disks come prepared for single-sided or double-sided use, depending upon the computer system. Also called diskette or floppy.

Disk backup. See Backup.

Disk-based WP
A WP that utilizes a disk to permanently store the current document in memory that is being edited. As changes are entered on screen, they are periodically written to disk as well. Disk-based WPs can handle larger documents than memory-based programs, since a disk ordinarily holds more data than the memory of a computer. (In some cases, a computer with additional memory boards may sometimes hold more memory than a disk. An IBM or compatible system, for example, with additional bytes, can provide up to 640K, while a double-sided floppy disk has a capacity of only 360K.) Single-sided disks provide space for more than 150,000 bytes; double-sided disks can hold well over 300,000. See also Memory-based WP.

Disk capacity
The amount of text, the number of text files, or the number of text pages that can be stored on one floppy disk. Page-oriented WPs store text on disks by pages. Therefore, a disk may hold 16 or 20 pages of text, depending upon

the WP. Document-oriented programs store text files differently on disks. Disk capacity is sometimes measured in K (kilobytes), as with the IBM system or in sectors by the Apple II machines. See also Disk space.

Disk command
A command that applies only to a disk. Directory or Catalog and Initialize or Format are simple disk commands. Others include Save, Load, Delete, and Replace. These commands usually require the name of the file and the disk drive number or letter to be entered.

Disk drive
An electronic device for recording and reading information stored on a disk. There are drives for "floppy" disks and for hard disks. (The latter store much more data, usually measured in megabytes.) A disk drive may be built into the computer or attached externally. Additional disk drives can often be added to a computer system.

Disk drive number
A method of differentiating between disk drives in a multiple-drive system. The standard procedure with Apple systems is to allocate Drive 1 for the program disk and Drive 2 for the data or destination disk. With IBM and compatible machines, the drives are labeled by letter, usually A, B, and C for a hard disk drive.

Disk full
A DOS message which appears on screen when a disk on which a file is to be stored has run out of space. To preserve the document or file, a new disk must be placed into the drive or some old files have to be deleted from the disk that is full.

Disk-resident storage system. See Disk-based
      WP.

Disk slot
The slot to which the disk drive interface
card is connected. The slot number depends on
the number of slots in the computer and the
recommendation of the computer manufacturer.
Two disk drives can each be connected to separate slots or both can be connected to the
same interface card. A hard disk drive must
have its own disk card.

Disk space
The amount of storage available for files. A
disk is divided into tracks, with each track
divided into sectors. Initialized disks reserve some space for DOS. The size of each
file is listed when the catalog or directory
is booted. The Apple computer system depicts
file size in sector number, while the PC DOS
and MS DOS systems list the size in bytes. See
also Disk capacity.

Diskette
The original term for the 5 1/4-inch magnetic
storage medium presently known as a "floppy"
disk. Some users reserve the term "diskette"
for the flexible model, while bestowing "disk"
on the hard or fixed storage device. The term
"diskette" seems to be waning in popularity in
favor of "disk." See also Disk.

Display
A device resembling a television screen, which
produces a visual representation of information, data, or graphics induced from a keyboard, a disk drive, a modem, or other peripheral. The display, sometimes called a monitor
or screen, can provide its information in
monochrome or in color. The most popular monochrome displays are available in either green
or amber with a black or dark background.

Monochrome is usually preferred over color when working with WPs. See also Display screen.

Display screen
A view or window which shows a particular amount of text, although more may be present in memory. The number of characters per line that are visible depends on the hardware and program. Some software displays 40 columns across; most WPs produce 80 columns. If more columns are present, they can be seen by a horizontal scroll feature. Display screens are often divided into specific areas. The command line or top line of the screen usually displays all menu options and prompts. The tab line generally informs the user of the present margin settings, tab stops, and line length. The work area (which sometimes includes a footnote section) holds the text that is edited, entered, deleted, formatted, etc. The status display or status line indicates the name of the file, the line number, the column number, the edit mode, etc. Sometimes the status line appears at the top of the screen.

Figure D.6   Sample Display Screen

```
 1) EDIT    2) SAVE    3) DELETE    4) PRINT
 ------------------------------------------------
 L::::T::::T::::T::::T::::T::::T::::T::R




              (WORK AREA)




 ------------------------------------------------
 DOCUMENT: SAMPLE   PAGE:12   LINE:7   COL:9
 ------------------------------------------------
```

61

Distributed processing system
The distribution of a computer system using multiple computers or processors interconnected by a communications network.

Document
In WPs, a unit of writing in the form of text stored under one file name. Some WPs distinguish between a document and a file. A document refers to a file in the memory of the computer and on the display screen. A file is a unit of information defined by one name and stored on a disk. Text files are loaded by the WP to the memory to form a document on screen. In other words, the impermanence of the screen text marks it as a document, while the file name and its storage on disk or tape characterize the information as a file. Other WPs use the two terms interchangeably. A document is sometimes called a file in memory.

Document assembly
Combining parts of documents or of the same document. Document assembly, another term for cut and paste, is performed by first marking blocks of text which are then copied and stored on disk. Each block is assigned its own file name. The blocks may be tables, paragraphs, or simply titles from other documents. Later, each block is joined to another to form or become part of a new document. Document assembly differs from block move. A block move is usually a single, temporary procedure, and the marked block of text is rarely saved for future use. See also Linking files, Merge.

Figure D.7   Example of Document Assembly

(text from Document A)

The average home buyer in the U.S. is 36 years old and married. He/she has a family income of approximately $42,000 and bought a house that cost about $75,000 with a down payment of approximately $14,000.

(data from Document B)

Mortgage Interest Rates Last Week

New York	11.07
New Jersey	10.80
California	11.50
Florida	10.09
Texas	11.25
Washington	10.50

(new document)

The average home buyer in the U.S. is 36 years old and married. He/she has a family income of approximately $42,000 and bought a house that cost about $75,000 with a down payment of approximately $14,000. To what extent do mortgage rates differ around the country? Here are the latest statistics:

Mortgage Interest Rates Last Week

New York	11.07
New Jersey	10.80
California	11.50
Florida	10.09
Texas	11.25
Washington	10.50

Document filing and retrieval. <u>See</u> Document.

Document insert
A method of inserting a block of text into a
document by first deleting it from another and
saving it, then replacing it into the original
before inserting it into another document.
This is an awkward procedure for a WP to use
in moving a block of text, especially when
other programs utilize an easier process, such
as simply making a copy of the text to be
moved. <u>See</u> <u>also</u> Block move, Boilerplating,
Document assembly.

Document-oriented WP
A type of WP which permits continuous pages of
text to be entered, depending upon the available memory. Programs such as Word Perfect,
SuperWriter, Perfect Writer, Word, WordStar,
and Volkswriter are document-oriented WPs in
that they allow an entire document to be edited at one time. Some of these programs show
page breaks, but they can be scrolled past
very quickly. In fact, a block of text that
has been split between two of these pages can
be marked and moved elsewhere while the page
break automatically readjusts itself. A document-oriented WP differs, in this sense, from
one that is page-oriented. <u>See</u> <u>also</u> Page-
oriented WP.

Document size limit
The length of a document a WP can handle on
screen. Document size limit may not be important for those who intend to use the program
for memos, letters, and reports of only a few
pages. But to the writer who works on full-
length books and long articles, size plays a
significant role in the selection of software.
WPs measure this capacity in different ways.
Programs such as Word Perfect, Word, and
Volkswriter are limited only by the capacity

of the disk. Perfect Writer and XyWrite II-
Plus base their size limit on the amount of
memory available by the computer. Some WPs
measure document size in terms of bytes. Thus,
MultiMate can handle up to 128K; SuperWriter,
32K; and WordStar 2000, 8MB. Still other programs list document size by the number of
pages or lines. Spellbinder, for example, has
a capacity of 10,000 lines, while PFS: Write
can manage 20 pages of text, and OfficeWriter,
256 pages.

Documentation
A manual of instructions for either a computer
or a program. Most WPs provide a printed documentation, although a few such as PC Write
feature their instructions on disk with an
option to have them printed out by the owner's
printer. Documentation may include tutorials,
instructions for configuring printers to work
with the WP, a "quick course" for those already experienced with WPs, a glossary, etc.

DOS
Abbreviation for disk operating system, which
provides instructions concerning the manage-
ment of files on a disk. Some important routines handled by DOS include loading and saving files, making certain they have names, and
checking available disk space. When DOS is
booted, the screen clears and the DOS prompt
appears, waiting to accept commands. These
commands include Catalog (for the Apple and
similar systems) or DIR (Directory, for IBM
and compatible machines). Either of these
commands lists on screen the contents of the
disk.

Figure D.8 DOS Commands for the
AppleWriter II

```
                DOS COMMANDS

           1. Catalog

           2. Rename File

           3. Lock File

           4. Unlock File

           5. Delete File

           6. Initialize diskette

      Enter your selection (1 - 6) :_
```

DOS format
Initializing a blank disk with the disk operating system so that the medium can store
files. Blanks must be formatted before they
can be used as storage or data disks.

Dot command
A command used with many WPs to format text. A
dot command consists of a period followed by a
series of characters embedded in the screen
text. These commands direct the printer to
perform particular functions. Although they
appear on the display screen, dot commands do
not print out on paper. Dot commands provide a
convenient approach to formatting a document.
Some WP programs use them to center a line of
text; to change the left margin, page lengths,
and page numbers; to omit page numbers; to
control the page number column; and to create
and store formats. See also Embedded command.

Figure D.9   Dot Commands for Header
and Page Number

```
        (as they appear on screen)

  .HE Chapter 2: Diversification

  .PN24

        (as they appear in print)

      Chapter 2: Diversification


            (text)


              24
```

Dot-matrix printer
A printer which uses a series of wire rods
embedded in a print head to create characters
or graphics. The daisy wheel, another type of
printer, uses fully formed characters whose
print is indistinguishable from that of a
conventional typewriter. Dot-matrix printers
are usually faster, can provide graphics, and
often cost less than daisy wheels. Dot matrix
printers can produce print ranging from data
to correspondence mode or near letter quality.
They can also print italics and other fonts as
well as type of various pitches. See also
Daisy wheel printer.

Double-column print. See Column mode.

Double density
A description of a magnetic storage medium
such as a disk that has been designed to
provide twice its storage capacity. This is
usually accomplished by utilizing finer mag-

netic particles which can hold twice the electronic charge of standard particles.

Double print. See Boldface.

Double space
A choice of line spacing offered by many WPs
during the printing process. In general, the
user can select from single- or double-spaced
formatting. Some WPs provide a wider choice of
line spacing. With some programs like Word-
Star, double space is selected before text is
entered. The line spacing then appears on
screen automatically during editing so that
the user can see each page and know the length
of the document as it will appear in print.

Double-strike mode
A printer function which produces a darker or
enhanced print on paper by having each character struck twice. Dot-matrix printers often
print in three modes: draft, double-strike,
and correspondence quality. Draft, or single-
strike mode, provides the lightest output but
prints the fastest. Double-strike or enhanced
mode is slower than draft but prints darker.
The best print mode, correspondence quality,
also prints the slowest. Double-strike differs
from correspondence quality: To achieve the
former, the printer may strike either the
vertical or horizontal dots only. In some
cases all dots are struck twice. With correspondence quality, the printer offsets the
printing head slightly so that the second
strike fills in the blank spaces between all
dots, giving each character a more solid appearance. See also Correspondence quality,
Draft mode.

Double underlining. See Underlining.

Double-width
A feature provided by many dot-matrix printers

which expands the pitch of the type or font. Double-width characters are generally used for headlines, titles, etc. The width is usually changed by adding special printer codes and works with pitches of 10, 12, or 17 characters per inch, or cpi.

Draft mode
A print mode which prints each character once. Draft print, or data processing mode, is used primarily for printing a document quickly regardless of the quality of the type. It is one feature of a dot-matrix printer offering several printing methods, including double-strike and correspondence quality. Draft print does not apply to daisy wheel printers, since these machines produce only one mode in terms of characters per second (cps) or speed. However, they do provide enhancements to their typewriter-like print, such as boldface, shadow print, etc. In dot-matrix printers, draft is the fastest, but lightest, mode, often printing at more than 160 to 180 characters per second, and sometimes even faster. See also Correspondence quality, Double-strike mode.

Dual intensity
The capability of a printer or computer terminal to print characters in both standard and bold (or highlighted) bright intensity formats. Boldface is more commonly applied to a printer function, which usually prints these characters twice so that they appear darker on the printed page. Highlighted or bright intensity characters refer to those on the display screen and are often used to emphasize menu headings, commands, etc. See also Boldface, Bright intensity, Normal intensity.

Duplicate text
A function included in many WPs for copying a block of text into a buffer or onto a disk so

that it can be inserted into another file or somewhere else in the same document. Also known as copy text. The process differs from document insert, an awkward procedure which requires that a block first be removed from a document, copied, and then replaced. See also Block move, Boilerplating.

Dvorak keyboard
An alternative keyboard layout of characters designed to increase typing speed and efficiency. The conventional pattern that can be found today on virtually all typewriters and computer keyboards is known as the Qwerty keyboard (after the first five keys of the top row of letters). It was originally intended to slow down the fast typists whose proficiency would cause the mechanical keys to jam on the early machines. The Dvorak system allegedly places the most often-used keys in more strategic positions. Today's electric and electronic keyboards can easily handle the accelerated typing speeds. Some WPs and other programs such as SmartKey II offer the user the option of reconfiguring the keyboard for personal use. Also, some keyboards provide the same option feature. See also Keyboard configuration, Qwerty keyboard.

Figure D.10   The Dvorak Keyboard Layout

```
    '  ,  .  P Y F G C R L /

    A O E U I D H T N S -

    ; Q J K X B M W V Z
```

E

e
The end edit command of Edlin, the DOS text
editor of IBM and similar computers. Entering
"e" stores the edited file and returns the
user to DOS. The command also changes the
extension of the unmodified file to BAK
(backup).

Edit
To alter or modify a file, document, etc.
Editing is one of the two basic functions of
all WPs, which always contain a text editor
and a text formatter. Programs provide special
editing features such as Insert, Remove, Move,
Search, and Replace. Editing features can
become very specific. Some WPs offer word,
line, sentence, and paragraph deletion; undelete; and column copy and move. Editing is
done with a cursor, a one-character symbol
navigated around the display screen, and
various keys. The cursor can be used to move
across text by word, by sentence, by paragraph, or by screen. It can also be moved to
the beginning or end of a line, screen, or
document. The more sophisticated the WP program, the more editing features it offers.

Figure E.1   Some Editing Features of a WP
      Designed for an IBM or Similar System

Arrow keys	move cursor one space in indicated direction
F1	displays edit help screen
F2	sets or clears tabs
F3	moves cursor to previous word
F4	moves cursor to next word
F5	deletes word left of cursor
F6	deletes word right of cursor
Home	moves cursor to beginning of document

Editing a document. See Document.

Editing defaults. See Default, Editor default.

Editing options
Choices a WP offers a user who wants to change a document in memory. These options, among others, may include adding a file or part of a file, copying or duplicating, deleting or removing, inserting or merging data from another file, moving a block of text, and searching and/or replacing text. Not all WPs provide all of the above. The higher-priced programs usually offer more features. See also Edit.

Figure E.2   Editing Menu of WordStar 2000

(Including Ruler Line)

```
^Blocks ^Tabs & Margins ^Print Enhancements

                                      ^Get Help

^Cursor      ^Locate Text      ^Remove    ^Undo

                                          ^Quit

^Options       ^Next Locate      ^Key Glossary


   ^G means hold down Ctrl key and press G

------2--^----3------4-------5------6------
```

Editor default
An editing parameter value previously assigned
by the WP program. Editor defaults usually
include the right margin, indentation, and tab
settings. WPs provide other default values
such as print default, etc. Editor default
values differ from print values in that the
former are permanently installed into the WP
and operate automatically, until they are
changed.   Print values, on the other hand, are
designated by the user and, in many cases,
must be re-entered each time the WP is booted
up.

Figure E.3   Editor Default Samples

```
Platen Width        =    8.0 inches

Left Margin         =    1.0 inch

Right Margin        =    1.0 inch

Characters Per Inch    =    10

Paper Length        =    11.0 inches

Top Margin          =    2.0 inches

Bottom Margin       =    2.0 inches

Lines per Inch      =    6
```

Eject
An embedded command provided by some WPs which informs the program to eject a printed page at any stage and to start a new page. The eject command is useful when the user is inserting a table, chart, or graph into a document on screen and it will not fit on one page. The command will force a paragraph or entire block of information to begin on the next page.

Electronic mail
The transmission of nonvoice messages from one computer to another through the use of telephone lines. Electronic mail is possible with partial or no physical movement of paper.

Electrostatic printer
A non-impact printer whose print head emits electric current into a specially designed ribbon. The ribbon heats up and melts onto the paper, forming characters. Electrostatic printers, which can produce letter-quality print, avoid the customary hammering noise of

impact printers. <u>See</u> <u>also</u> Non-impact printer, Printer.

Element
The interchangeable printing device, such as a thimble or daisy wheel, of a printer. The element contains the type font. <u>See</u> <u>also</u> Daisy wheel printer, Font, Thimble.

Elite
A style of type that measures 12 characters to the horizontal inch. Elite is the smaller of the two popular sizes of typewriter typefaces. Pica, the other typeface, measures 12 cpi. <u>See</u> <u>also</u> Font.

Embedded character
A character which appears in a text document on screen but is not printed on a page. Embedded characters are used to give instructions to the printer or the computer. They are sometimes, but not necessarily, preceded by a period at the beginning of a line. These are called dot commands. <u>See</u> <u>also</u> Dot command, Embedded command.

Embedded command
An instruction given to the computer or printer and placed directly into the document. Embedded commands, like embedded characters, are installed into the text and are visible on screen, but they do not appear during the printouts of hard copy. They are an easy method of changing space, line, and other functions without resorting to alternate menus during text entry. Some WPs do not use embedded commands for such functions as underlining, boldface, etc. Instead, they appear directly on screen in reverse video. One advantage of this is that the document more closely resembles what will eventually be printed on paper.

Figure E.4   Embedded Commands

(as they appear on screen)

Some WPs require the use of ^Uem-
bedded commands^U to perform such tasks
as ^Uunderlining^U, ^Bboldface^B, etc.

(as they appear in print)

Some WPs require the use of
embedded commands to perform such
tasks as underlining, **boldface**, etc.

Embedded ruler
Placing a ruler or ruler line in the text for
the purpose of altering margins. Most WPs
provide default margins for the left and right
sides of the page. These parameters are sometimes displayed by an on-screen ruler.   Using
an embedded ruler is one of the various methods of changing the default values. Some programs permit the insertion of embedded rulers.
This can prove useful in designing charts and
tables, entering quotations from other files,
etc. See also Ruler line.

End key
A key on the numeric keypad of a keyboard that
moves the cursor to the bottom of a document,
which may be longer than the text appearing on
screen. In many WPs, the function is performed
by pressing the control key before the end key
is depressed.

End-of-paragraph symbol
A sign placed next to the end of a paragraph
or in the right margin, signifying that the
user would like to start a new paragraph. Some
WPs such as WordStar, Volkswriter, and Easywriter provide for the use of end-of-paragraph

symbols, while others do not. These symbols, which vary from a musical note, the number sign, a paragraph sign, or a "smaller than" sign, are entered automatically whenever the enter or return key is pressed.

Figure E.5   Sample End-of-Paragraph Symbols

> Some WPs use these end-of-paragraph symbols by placing them at the end of a line of text whenever the enter or return key is pressed.   <
> This designates the end of one paragraph and the beginning of another.   <

Endnote
An alternate placement of a footnote. Endnotes are located at the end of documents, in the same formal arrangement as footnotes. Some WPs offer the user a choice of placing citations on the bottom of a page or at the end of the entire report; others provide only the latter feature. The more sophisticated packages handle both footnotes and endnotes automatically, to the extent of changing the call number or letter each time a reference is added or deleted. See also Footnoting.

Enhanced print
A print mode of a dot-matrix printer in which each character is struck twice, thereby producing a somewhat darker print. Also known as double-strike, enhanced print is slower than single-strike or draft mode but faster than correspondence quality print. See also Correspondence quality, Double-strike mode, Print enhancement.

Enhanced printing
A mode used by a dot-matrix printer to produce
a darker printout. Enhanced printing empha-
sizes characters more than draft print mode,
but not as much as correspondence quality, the
best mode of this type of printer. The speed
at which these three modes operate varies,
depending on the printer. For instance, if the
machine can produce up to 160 characters per
second (cps) in draft mode, then it usually
provides 80 cps in enhanced mode and 40 cps in
correspondence quality.

Enhancement
A method of emphasizing or accepting portions
of text in a document to show that they have
been specially treated. For example, some WPs
display boldface, underlining, and blocks of
text in inverse video. Enhancement may apply
to menu items, commands, etc. See also Print
enhancement.

Figure E.6   Example of Enhancement

> Enhancement is useful if certain
> **headings** or individual **words** are to
> be emphasized.

Enter
To type any data or information on the keyboard. Also, the most important key on a computer keyboard. The enter key usually performs
various functions such as sending information
to the computer, giving the computer instructions, marking the end of a paragraph, etc.
Menu options usually require the user to make
a selection and then press Enter or Return.

Envelope printing option
A feature offered by many business-oriented

WPs which print the address from a letter onto an envelope. In some cases, the program directs the user to place the envelope into the printer; the WP then orders the printer to move the envelope 10 lines down, 35 spaces across, and print the desired address.

Erase a file. See Delete, Remove.

Error message
A method employed by WPs to warn the user why the system will not perform a selected function. Disk Full, I/O Error, Syntax Error, File-Type Mismatch, and File Not Found are some typical error messages. Corrections consist of pressing Return or Enter, using DOS commands, pressing Escape, etc.

Escape key
A much-used function key, often used to cancel a command or option or to return to editing, the main menu, etc. Some functions the escape key can usually cancel are Copy, Delete, Format, Highlight, Insert, Move, Merge, Page Length, Replace, Search, and Spell Check. With some WPs, pressing the escape (ESC) key returns the program to the previous function or screen. Whatever function is activated or deactivated by this key, it can prevent many disasters.

Exit function
A procedure for leaving a WP program and returning to DOS. Before exiting from a program, it is usually necessary to return to the main menu. Entering DOS may be useful for several reasons. The user may wish to perform various DOS commands or load a different program into the computer memory. Some WP programs warn the user before exiting that the latest document in memory has not been saved. Many WPs recommend leaving by way of the exit option rather than just shutting the power off.

Exit to DOS. <u>See</u> Exit function.

Extension
A code that composes the second half of a file name as applied to IBM and compatible systems. The extension usually consists of three letters preceded by a period. It is often descriptive and designed to help define the file contents: e.g., LTR for letter, PGM for program, TST for test, NTS for notes, etc.

Figure E.7   Extension Samples

```
(file names without extensions)

            BUDGET1
            MARKETA
            MARKETB
            HISTORY

(file names with extensions)

            BUDGET.FEB
            BUDGET.MAR
            BUDGET.APR
            MARKET.RPT
            MARKET.LTR
            HISTORY.TST
            HISTORY.NTS
            NOTES.DOC
```

External memory
A storage device used in conjunction with a WP for holding information or data. External memory can be a soft or floppy disk, a hard disk, or a cassette tape. External memory is permanent, whereas computer memory or Random Access Memory is temporary. When the power of the computer is shut off, all information in its RAM is gone forever. Simply because valu-

able information is stored on a permanent medium such as any one of the above examples of external memory, there is no reason to be overly optimistic about its security. Because disks can be lost or damaged, it is prudent to back up all stored information.

External storage. <u>See</u> External memory.

F

File

A document containing a collection of records
or data, all with the same format, which has
been saved onto a disk under one file name.
Files must be given a name before they are
stored on disk. There are different kinds of
files, including text files created by WPs,
database files, program files, etc. A text
file cannot be booted by the DOS system; it
can only be loaded to the screen through a WP
program. Various WPs have different limitations concerning names of files and their
lengths. Some provide extensions consisting of
a period and three characters. See also File
name, Text file.

File chaining

A feature on some WPs which links preselected
files on disk to be printed automatically in
sequence. The procedure, as used by programs
such as PFS: Write, usually involves inserting
a command at the end of each file. This nota-
tion prepares the next file for printing. File
chaining is an expedient way of printing a
series of documents without configuring each
one separately. WPs using this function use
the format of the first file as the default
parameters for those that follow.

File directory. <u>See</u> Directory.

File in memory. <u>See</u> Document.

File merge. <u>See</u> Merge.

File name
A method of identifying a document so that it can be saved, loaded into memory, and distinguished from other files. Each WP imposes its own restrictions on file name length, types of characters which can be used, etc. For example, some permit up to 15 characters to be used, while others limit a name to eight. Some allow spaces between words; others do not. Still others permit three-character extensions to file names, as long as they are preceded by a period. This helps to identify the type of file: e.g., Jones.ltr or Sanders.rpt distinguishes between letters and reports. Some users simplify their file-tracking system by using the following technique: RESEARCH1, RESEARCH2, etc. File name is sometimes written as "filename."

Figure F.1 File Name Samples

CUMMINGS RPT 1 (Appleworks: allows 15
    characters, spaces, numbers, etc.)

GEOLOGY-TEST1 (MultiMate: allows 20
    numbers, letters; no punctuation,
    spaces)

MATTHEWS.LTR (IBM: allows 8 letters,
    numbers; 3-letter extension; no
    spaces)

File name extension. See Extension.

File not found
An error message which appears on screen when the system cannot locate a file whose name is typed. Some common mistakes which lead to this message include typing errors, insertion of the wrong disk into the drive, and failure to type the file name extension.

File size
The amount of space permitted for each text file. Some WPs use a memory-based system which is dependent upon the maximum memory of the computer. This machine memory, however, is not all devoted to text files. For instance, a computer with 128K (kilobytes), after allowing for the storage of the WP itself and some housekeeping chores, may offer only 55K for text. These WPs often have severe file size limitations, ranging from seven to 26 pages in many instances. This restriction, however, may not affect certain uses, such as letter writing, small reports, or term papers for school. Other WPs utilize virtual memory, a system which includes the disk storage space. This method provides over 100K for single-sided disks and well over 300K for double-sided disks. WPs that use virtual memory are limited in file size only by their disk capacity. See also Disk-based WP, Virtual memory.

File space
The number of characters in a file. File space, and size, depend on the computer system. A machine with 64K (64,000 bytes) obviously handles fewer characters than a computer with 256K bytes.

File system menu
A list of file options provided by most WPs and printed on the screen. A file system menu differs from other menus in one major area: it

allows the user to work with or manipulate files. Main menus, on the other hand, offer a wider choice of topics, including the use of spelling checkers; other submenus provide different functions, such as printer installation routines, color monitor use, etc.

Figure F.2   A Sample File System Menu

```
1- GET A FILE

2- EDIT A FILE

3- DELETE A FILE

4- SAVE A FILE

5- PRINT A FILE
```

File-to-file access
The ability of a WP to permit text from one file to be entered into another, usually an on-screen document. File-to-file access allows a second file, usually stored on disk, to be joined to the document that is on screen and at the cursor position. This lets the user combine two different files or ideas into one complete thought. The process can be a rather simple one or a complex series of multiple files joined into a complete report. See also Boilerplating.

File type mismatch
An error message which appears on screen in conjunction with certain WPs and is caused by trying to load nontext files. WPs utilize file type mismatch when the user attempts to give a formatted file a name already attributed to an unformatted file.

Filter
A program designed to convert particular WP
text files into standard ASCII files. Some WP
programs such as PFS: Write save their files
on disk with no line-feed characters or symbols; these files, therefore, are not compatible with other software programs unless a
filter program is utilized.

Find
A WP feature designed to locate a word or
phrase in a document. Find can usually operate
backward as well as forward. Sometimes it is
part of the search and replace function. Some
WP programs make a distinction between upper-
and lower-case letters. Aside from its basic
function of locating a word or phrase, the
find feature can be (and usually is) used for
replacing text. See also Global search and
replace, Search and replace.

Figure F.3   Example of Using Find

```
        [F]ind:   /door/


      The police sergeant stopped the man
  at the _door. "I'd like to have a word
  with you."

            (_ = cursor)
```

Firmware
Programs that often accompany the computer and
are supplied by the manufacturer; also, software stored on chips. Various operating systems are considered firmware. A manufacturer
may offer CP/M along with its own system,
since CP/M allows access to a wide variety of
software applications that can be used with

the computer. Other examples of firmware include PRODOS and MS DOS. Some firmware can be
purchased separately as an accessory item.
Many companies offer CP/M as an adjunct to
Apple owners.

Fixed disk. see Hard disk.

Fixed escapement
A term applied to printers that allot an equal
amount of space to every character regardless
of the differences in the width of each. Fixed
escapement printers treat the characters "i"
and "m" as if they were the same width. This
produces more white space to the right and
left of some characters than it does in the
case of others. Fixed escapement is found on
virtually all conventional typewriters. Some
printers, however, are capable of microjustification, which controls the amount of white
space on both sides of each character, depending on its width. Some WPs support this
feature, which produces hard copy similar to
typeset copy. See also Microjustification,
Proportional spacing.

Flagging. See Alphabetical indexing.

Flexible disk. See Floppy disk.

Floppy disk
A flexible plastic substance containing a
magnetic coating and used as a storage medium
for data or information. A floppy disk consists of a protective jacket, a reinforced hub
ring, stress relief notches, a read/write
window, an index/timing hole, a write-protect
notch, and a specifications label. Floppy
disks usually come in hard- or soft-sector
versions and in different sizes, the most
popular being 5 1/4 inches and 8 inches. Floppy disks can be removed from the disk drive,
unlike many hard disks. Some floppies store

information on only one side (single side),
while others can be written on both (double
side). Unlike a phonograph record, which has a
spiral groove, the floppy consists of invisi-
ble concentric circles called tracks.

Flush right
The alignment of text with the right margin,
except for paragraph endings. Not all WPs
provide this feature. All have flush left, of
course, and many have flush right, especially
the more costly products. Some programs equate
the term "flush right" with full justification, i.e., flush left and right margins. However, the term is more widely, and, appropriately, used to indicate a ragged left margin.
See also Right justification.

Figure F.4   Example of Flush Right

> Sometimes flush right is used for
> special effects, especially in the
> design of bulletins
> and other such publications and
> printed matter. The result is striking
> and different, and
> therefore eye-catching.

Font
The type style in which text is printed. Elite
and pica, two kinds of font, differ only in
size. Roman and Gothic fonts differ in style,
the former consisting of thick and thin lines,
the latter of lines of equal thickness. Most
WPs permit the changing of font, depending
upon the capabilities of the printer. Dot-
matrix printers, for instance, can produce
double-width characters, bold print, italics,
etc. Many of these printers allow the user to
create custom fonts or purchase ready-made

ones from commercial vendors. Daisy wheel
printers provide unlimited fonts, relying on
various print wheels which can easily be inserted into the printer. Some WPs such as Word
display various type fonts on screen. See also
Pitch.

Footer
One or more lines of data or information appearing at the bottom of a page exclusive of
the body of text. Footers may consist of
dates, titles, page numbers, etc. Usually,
however, they are used to display page numbers. Therefore, many WPs provide footers
whose page numbers automatically increase in
increments of one. Footers can be formatted to
appear on the left or right side or in the
center of the bottom line of a page. See also
Header.

Footnote options menu
The part of a WP that lets the user select the
type of call symbol and the arrangement of
footnotes numbers. Some call symbol options
include characters, letters, or numbers. Footnote numbering options include using cumula-
tive numbers throughout the document or numbers that start anew on each page. See also
Footnoting.

Footnoting
The ability of a WP to place references at the
bottom of a page of text or collect them and
place them at the end of a document. Different
WPs provide various means to accomplish this.
One technique uses embedded commands in the
text. The program is then directed to remove
the phrase and position it at the bottom of
the page. Some WPs permit up to 15 footnotes
to appear on a single page. Other programs
provide an option which places the footnotes
in order after the last page of a document is
printed. See also Endnote.

Foreground mode
A function of certain WPs which allows the
user to edit text to a document on screen
while another is being printed. These programs
offer two modes, foreground and background,
the latter being the one contained in a
"spooler," a holding device which permits the
WP and the computer to continue working with
another document. See also Background mode.

Foreign-language keyboard
A feature that permits the creation of foreign
characters. WPs use several methods to generate this function. Volkswriter, for instance, combines the alternate key and an
alphabetic key; Samna Word III allows the user
to reconfigure the entire keyboard to simulate
French, Spanish, German, Italian, and other
languages.

Form feed
A function that sends a command to the printer
when a page has been printed. The command
informs the printer to eject the page or, in
the case of a cut-sheet feeder, to load a new
sheet of paper.

Form length
The size of the sheet of paper on which the
document or file is to be printed. The standard length is 11 inches (8 1/2 X 11 inches)
or 66 lines. This is usually the default value
set by the WP or the printer. The form length
can be altered by the user through either the
printer or the WP program. Sometimes form
length is known as document page length.

Figure F.5   Example of Form Length
as Part of a Print Options Menu

```
LINES PER INCH              6

NUMBER OF COPIES            1

START AT PAGE NUMBER        1

LINES PER PAGE             55

FORM LENGTH                66

         Press Enter to accept
                  or
      Press Tab Key to each number
             to change default
```

Format
To prepare or initialize a new, blank, or used
disk for the disk operating system or a WP
system. If a disk is not formatted, documents
created by a WP as well as programs cannot be
saved and stored on it. Formatting a disk
through DOS includes two specific procedures.
First, the operating system format is written
on the disk. Next, the major portion of the
system is placed on the same disk. When the
computer is turned on, the disk drive is activated and the operating system is loaded into
RAM. A disk formatted for one WP does not
necessarily mean it can be used with another.
Formatting erases any files previously stored
on that disk. Some WPs provide a utility within their program for the purpose of formatting
a disk, a useful feature when a current data
disk becomes full and another is required.
Other WPs require that the disk be formatted
externally before text is stored. With these
programs, a supply of disks should be prepared
in advance.

Format command
An instruction to the WP, usually created by
the control key and a letter, which aligns the
text for printing the document in a predetermined arrangement. Some format commands
include margins, indentations, and quotations.
Format commands are sometimes inserted directly into the text on screen. Some WPs, like The
Write Stuff, provide the options of displaying
the format on screen, saving the commands, and
recalling them at will.

Figure F.6   Some Format Commands
for WordStar

CONTROL OL	SET LEFT MARGIN
CONTROL OR	SET RIGHT MARGIN
CONTROL OX	RELEASE MARGINS
CONTROL OI	SET TAB
CONTROL ON	CLEAR TAB
CONTROL OS	SET LINE SPACING
CONTROL OC	CENTER TEXT

Format conversion. See Converting text files.

Format file
A list of settings used to configure a document. The typical format file controls such
items as justification, margins, lines per
page, tabs, hyphenation, etc. Format files,
which can be changed to conform to a user's
particular needs, usually do away with embedded dot commands, which are placed within the

text on screen but do not appear in the final printout. With some WPs the format file can be altered from within the editing mode, while others must be changed through the opening or main menu. Depending on the WP, a document with one format may not be printed under the format file of another document. The second has to be altered to conform to the original. Format files simplify the process of arranging text.

Format mask
A method offered by some WPs for creating and saving a form with preset definitions. Format masks can be set up for office memos, form letters, shipping orders, reports, or other standard forms. Once the tabs, page length, margins, headings, openings, and closings are defined, they can be saved for future use so that each form is standardized. For example, in creating a format mask for a business letter, the user establishes where the date, address and closing will be located. WPs such as PowerText identify and locate these elements, making the production of formatted documents relatively easy. Surprisingly, some of the more costly WP programs have neglected to include this useful feature. See also Style sheet.

Format options
A feature offered by many WPs to aid in the arrangement of the printed page. By setting text and form size in advance, the user does not have to make any further adjustments during word processing. Format options, such as those designed for letters, labels, and memos, can be saved for use with future documents. Typical options include those for length, width, and spacing.

Figure F.7   Examples of Format Options

```
NUMBER OF LINES PER PAGE          ___
LINE SPACING (1, 2, 3)            ___
LEFT MARGIN                       ___
RIGHT MARGIN                      ___
JUSTIFICATION (L, R, F)           ___
TOP MARGIN                        ___
BOTTOM MARGIN                     ___
```

Format text
To move one or more lines of text to the right
or left margin or to the center of a page. WPs
provide various methods for formatting text.
Some of the more popular procedures employed
include menu prompts, control or function key
commands, or embedded commands. PFS: Write,
for example, makes formatting text a simple
task by offering, through a function key, a
choice of L (Left), R (Right), or C (Centering
the line). AppleWriter II, on the other hand,
uses dot commands with characters, e.g., cj
(center justify) and lj (left justify). See
also Center a line.

Figure F.8   Example of Formatting Text

```
            (as it appears on screen)

.cj
A STREETCAR NAMED DESIRE
By Tennessee Williams
.lj

            (as it appears in print)

            A STREETCAR NAMED DESIRE
              By Tennessee Williams
```

Formatted file
A duplicate copy of a typed document, including tab stops, margins, spacing, etc. A formatted file usually implies a document stored on disk. With some WPs, formatted files cannot be divided and transferred to other files.

Formed character printer
An impact printer that is capable of producing fully formed type through the use of a ribbon. There are two kinds of formed character printers, each using a different printing element: the daisy wheel, as employed by such companies as Diablo, Qume, and Juki; and the thimble, used by NEC. Each of these printing elements contains a set of fully formed characters that are used to strike a ribbon to produce printing. The letter-quality print resembles the print of a good typewriter. See also Daisy wheel printer, Impact printer, Printer, Thimble.

Full justification
Text that extends evenly to both the left and right margins. Many WPs provide various options to justify text. Documents can be center justified as well as left and right justified. Right justification is sometimes used to mean full justification, since some WPs use the former term to describe text whose left and right margins are even. However, in the strictest sense, text with left justification implies that its right column will appear ragged, and conversely, right justification suggests that its left column will remain ragged. Text is usually justified by adding spaces between words on each line.

Full-screen editor
A WP that provides almost the entire display screen for the editing of text. Some programs use the top half of the screen for a main menu

of options, while other WPs devote a few top
and bottom lines for various options. Software
such as The Final Word offers full-screen
editing, except for one line of information at
the bottom of the screen. This feature can be
a mixed blessing. One advantage is that the
user can see more text at one time; another is
that there is less clutter and distraction
while typing or editing. On the other hand,
the user may have to resort to the help menu
frequently, and this can be annoying. Most WPs
utilize full-screen editing.

Figure F.9   Example of Full-Screen Display

```
A:FILENAME   PAGE 1   LINE 1   COL 3   INS ON

L---|---|---|---|---|---|---|---|---|---R
  -



              (text)
```

Function
An operation or feature of a WP. WPs perform
numerous functions, which fall into two major
categories: editing and formatting. Editing
functions include, among others, Insert, Delete, Move, Load, and Save. Formatting functions affect the way the document will look on
paper and include justification, margins, and
underlining. Functions are activated by pres-

sing a keyboard character suggested by a menu
or by pressing multiple keys such as a function key and a character key. The more sophisticated the program, the more functions available to the user.

Function key
A dedicated keyboard key designed to perform
only one task. The purpose of function keys is
to shorten commands and save keystrokes. IBM
and similar computers have 10 function keys,
usually numbers from F1 to F10, located to the
left of the main keyboard. Some manufacturers
place as many as 15 function keys across the
top of the keyboard. Other computer companies
such as Apple do not supply any numbered function keys on their keyboards. Function keys
are usually employed for such tasks as deleting words, moving blocks of text, calling up a
help menu to the screen, and moving the cursor
to the top or bottom of a document. They
differ from special function keys such as
Control, Alternate, Print Screen, Page Up,
etc. See also Special function key.

Figure F.10 Some Function Keys
Used by PFS: Write

F1   Displays the type/edit help screen

F2   Sets and clears tab stops

F3   Moves cursor to previous word

F4   Moves cursor to next word

G

Get document. _See_ Load.

Get page/go to page. _See_ Page-down key,
Page-up key.

Global editing. _See_ Global search and replace.

Global find. _See_ Find, Global search and
replace.

Global search and replace
The ability of a WP to search through a document for a character, a word, or a group of
words and, if desired, to automatically replace all or part of that text with other
text. Global search and replace should be used
with caution. Part of the text not intended to
be altered may be replaced. The user may want
to change all "ands," for example, to the "&"
symbol, but may forget to include blank spaces
before and after the word at the prompt sign.
This may result in such words as "band" or
"brand," which include the letters "and" being
changed unintentionally. Global search and
replace usually includes the option of locating a single occurrence, which can then be
changed at the user's discretion.

```
WORD(S) TO FIND: word processor

REPLACE WITH: WP

OPTIONS:  (1- STOP AT EACH OCCURRENCE)
          (2- REPLACE ALL OCCURRENCES)
          (3- IGNORE CASE)
          (4- CANCEL COMMAND)

SELECT ONE: 2
```

Glossary
A method of storing often-repeated words,
phrases, or names which can then be easily
retrieved and loaded anywhere into a document
on screen. WPs such as Word and Applewriter II
can produce temporary as well as permanent
glossaries which, with two or three keystrokes, can print phrases and difficult-to-
type names into documents on screen. The glossary is a time- and labor-saving feature. Some
WP programs refer to this function by other
names, including key glossary, library, or
macro. See also Key file, Key procedure.

Glue line
An editing function which moves text up from
the line below to the line the cursor is on.
Usually, the amount of text which moves up is
limited only by the space available up to the
right margin. During this procedure the cursor
(_) can reside anywhere along the line.

Figure G.2   Example of Glue Line

```
            (before)

    There are many uses for this
function.
One purpose is to remove super-
fluous blank spaces.


            (after)

    There are many uses for this
function. One purpose is to remove
superfluous blank spaces.
```

Glue paragraph
A function of some WPs such as Magic Window II
which brings together an entire paragraph
using only one command. This feature is similar to glue line, but works with more than a
single line at a time.

Figure G.3   Example of Glue Paragraph

```
            (before)

    Sometimes sentences belonging to
one paragraph are broken
up during the editing process.
The purpose of glue paragraph is to re-
unite them into a unified paragraph.


            (after)

    Sometimes sentences belonging to
one paragraph are broken up during the
editing process. The purpose of glue
paragraph is to reunite them into a
unified paragraph.
```

Grammar checker

A program designed to check text files of WPs for grammatical errors, etc. Grammar checkers search documents for archaic words, errors in capitalization and punctuation, words typed twice by mistake, redundant phrases or words, etc. Some of these checkers also provide word counts, such as the number of words in sentences, the number of times phrases such as "to be" have been used in a document, etc. See also Spelling checker.

Graph printing

The ability of a WP to incorporate a graph or chart from another program into a document so that it can be printed as a complete document. Some programs such as PFS: Write allow graphs to be inserted from PFS: Graph, part of the PFS family of programs, as well as from other sources.

Graphics

Specially constructed designs, such as bar graphs, charts, and circles, produced by a computer sytem or a WP. Some WP programs can retrieve graphics from other software and add them to a document. For example, PFS: Write allows the user to add charts and graphs from PFS: Graph, a related program. To print graphics, the user must have a dot-matrix or similar printer. See also Graph printing.

H

Half line spacing
A feature of some WPs such as MultiMate that places printed lines a half line apart. See also Double space, Vertical spacing.

Hanging paragraph
A paragraph of text whose first line begins at the left margin, while succeeding lines are indented. Hanging paragraphs are used in creating reports containing detailed outlines and in posters and brochures. See also Indentation, Outdent.

Figure H.1   Example of Hanging Paragraphs

    There are many applications for which the hanging paragraph is well suited:

It can be applied to those occasions in which a special report requires detailed outlines.

It is also useful in designing posters in which particular points are to be emphasized (date, time, etc.).

Hard copy
Any text, document, data, or information
printed on paper. The printing device may be a
dot-matrix or daisy wheel printer or an electronic typewriter interfaced for use with a
computer. The term may also refer to part of a
command, such as "Print Hard Copy," informing
the computer system that a printout on paper
is desired. See also Copy.

Hard disk
A magnetic-coated rigid platter which rotates
in an enclosed housing and is used for storing
and playing back data, information, or programs on a computer screen. Hard disk drives
are either built into computers or attached
externally. Hard disks generally hold much
more information than their "floppy" counter-
parts. A 10MB hard disk drive, for example,
can store data equivalent to 30 5 1/4-inch
disks. Hard disks tend to feed data to the
screen at a much faster rate than soft disks.
Also, hard disks ordinarily are "fixed" in
place; i.e., they cannot be removed from the
drive, as can floppy disks.

Hard hyphen
A hyphen symbol that is permanently embedded
in the text and that will not be deleted if
text in which it appears is reformatted. The
more sophisticated WPs produce two types of
hyphens, soft and hard. The soft hyphen is
used at line endings to divide words, giving a
better appearance to the printed page. If a
paragraph is reformatted, soft hyphens disap-
pear if they occur anywhere other than at the
end of a line. Hard hyphens, on the other
hand, are permanent and are used for grammatical reasons or between names (cross-examine,
Tri-Micro Products, Lord Hyde-White). See
Hyphenation, Soft hyphen.

Figure H.2   The Hard Hyphen

```
(hard hyphen followed by soft hyphen)

    The witness protested the cross-
examination by the prosecuting at-
torney.

    (reformatted with hard hyphen intact
     and soft hyphen eliminated)

    The stubborn witness protested the
cross-examination by the prosecuting
attorney.
```

Hard return
The use of the enter or return key at the end of a line or paragraph. A hard return is similar to a carriage return on a conventional typewriter. Most WPs differentiate between a line return (soft return) or word wrap and the end of a paragraph. In fact, many WPs mark the hard return with a symbol to the right of the line, where the paragraph ends and the new one is to begin. Hard returns are important in reformatting paragraphs following editing. See also Word wrap.

Hard space
A space inserted between two closely related words to prevent them from being separated and placed on different lines during paragraph reformatting, etc. The user may want groups of terms or words such as "Mr. Smith" or "Washington, D.C." to be kept on the same line. The more sophisticated WPs such as WordStar provide this feature. Hard spaces are usually activated through a control key.

Hardware
Any electronic device or instrument, either
internal or external, used in conjunction with
a computer. The computer itself, and its various components, including the terminal, keyboard, disk drives, and printer are examples
of hardware. See also Firmware, Software.

Header
A line or more of text at the top of the page
exclusive of the body of text. The header may
be a title of a document, a subheading, a page
number, etc. Not all WPs offer this feature
which, when formatted, will appear on each
page of a document. Setting up a header requires more effort than simply adding text to
a document. Either special menus or commands
handle this task and include such options as
placing the header to the left or right or in
the center of the page. It can also include
both a title and a page number, each placed in
different positions at the top of each sheet.
See also Footer.

Help menu
A quick method of obtaining assistance without
the user's having to resort to the documentation of a WP. Some programs offer extensive
help menus in the areas of editing, formatting, printing, etc. Others give very little
help information on screen, either because of
the simplicity of the program or by deliberate
design. Some WPs such as WordStar provide the
option of making the help screens visible
throughout the editing process or removing
them from the screen. In some cases, they
occupy a large portion of the screen and can
be distracting as well as helpful.

Figure H.3   Sample Help Screen

```
        1. Cursor Movement

        2. Delete/Retrieve Text

        3. Tabs

        4. Saving a File

        5. Loading a File

        6. Embedded Print Commands

        7. Printing a File


    ENTER YOUR SELECTION: (1 - 7) _
```

Highlighting
A feature offered by some WPs in which portions of text written on the screen are made
more prominent through the use of light intensity. Highlighting can be presented in various
colors with a color terminal. Highlighting is
sometimes used in conjunction with screen
menus to emphasize items such as file names.

HMI. See Horizontal motion index.

Home key
A special function key on IBM and compatible
keyboards designed to move the cursor to the
beginning of a document on screen. Not all WPs
use the home key similarly. Some use it alone
for one function and in combination with another key for a different function. See also
End key.

Home word processor
A euphemism for an inexpensive WP with limited
features. Bank Street Writer is an example of
a home WP. Because its major instructions
appear on screen, it can be used as soon as it
is booted up. It does not have the capabilities of programs such as Peachtext, WordStar,
or MultiMate, which can access companion programs such as spelling checkers, mail merge,
and index programs. Home WPs, which include
such basic features as Insert, Erase, and
Print, are useful for writing letters, school
reports, notes, etc.

Horizontal motion index
A feature of some WPs designed to set the
amount of space between characters. Horizontal
motion index, or HMI, works only with printers
capable of movements in increments of 1/120 of
an inch between characters. HMI is important
when working with microjustification and true
proportional spacing. Some WPs have a default
value of 10 (10 characters per inch, or cpi),
others, 11 cpi. See also Microjustification,
True proportional spacing.

Horizontal scroll
The ability to view a screen with lines of
text wider than 80 columns. Most WPs provide
for scrolling up and down, but only a few
programs offer horizontal scrolling. This
ability to move the screen over the text from
left to right and then back is useful for
editing wider documents and for viewing
spreadsheets. See also Scroll, Vertical
scroll.

Horizontal slide
A function of some WPs designed to move words
or parts of a line to the left or right. Words
or portions of a line are moved one space at a
time along a line of text. Horizontal slide is
ordinarily accomplished by placing the cursor
in position and pressing either the space bar,
backspace, or delete key.

Horizontal spacing. See Horizontal motion
        index.

Hotline
A telephone number set up by a WP company to
assist a registered user who may be having
difficulty with the program. Companies vary in
the length of time their hotline remains in
effect, such as three or six months. Some
limit the hours they are available, while
others maintain a 24-hour service.

Housekeeping activities
 A term referring to certain commonplace but
useful functions which expedite working with a
WP. Some housekeeping activities include copying text files, renaming files, deleting
files, formatting disks, converting files so
that they work with other programs, and printing. Some WPs store these functions in separate utility files or programs. WPs generally
provide three types of functions: (a) creating
or editing a document, (b) housekeeping activities, and (c) other utilities such as spell
check, printer installation, modification of
default values, and disk drive control. See
also Utility program.

Figure H.4   Sample Housekeeping Activities

```
ADDITIONAL FUNCTIONS SUBMENU

    1. Load Tab File

    2. Save Tab File

    3. Load Glossary File

    4. Save Glossary File

    5. Connect Keyboard to Printer

    6. Quit

Enter selection (1-6) and Press Return:_
```

Hyphenation
A method used to combine or divide words and
terms. There are two kinds of hyphenation:
hard, or permanent, hyphens (examples: cross-
examine, self-reliant); and soft, or temporary
hyphens, which occur when words are artifi-
cially divided by a line break. Since most WPs
utilize word wrap, which automatically moves
words to the right and down to the next line
as text is added to a document, the problem is
how to keep the hard hyphens intact and how to
eliminate the soft hyphens when text is added,
edited, or reformatted. Some more sophisticated programs provide a feature called automatic or semi-automatic hyphenation, in which
the user is requested to hyphenate a word so
that a particular line will conform to a pre-
arranged margin. Hyphenation is most useful
when text has to be full- or right-justified;
it helps to eliminate excessive white space on
the printed page. See also Hard hyphen, Proportional spacing, Soft hyphen.

Hyphenation–assist
A feature of some WPs designed to help keep
the right margin of a document relatively even
without justification. In some typing situations an unusually long word, when moved to
the next line, leaves an untidy blank space on
the text line. With the hyphenation-assist
feature the cursor appears on the word. The
user then has the option of using a hyphen or
not with each of these words. See also Hard
hyphen, Soft hyphen.

Figure H.5 Hyphenation-Assist

(before)

When a long word such as
"hyphenation" does not fit on one line,
a large gap appears. This feature
permits the word to be hyphenated to
fill in the blank space.

(hyphenation-assist options)

1. To hyphenate, press -
2. You may move cursor left or right
   to change location of hyphen
3. If no hyphen is desired, press
   Escape

(after option 1)

When a long word such as "hyphenation" does not fit on one line, a large
gap appears. This feature permits the
word to be hyphenated to fill in the
blank space.

I

Icon
A visual drawing or representation describing
a computer function. Icons, used with WPs such
as HomeWord, may consist of a file cabinet for
storage or retrieval, a pair of scissors for
editing, a printer for hard copy, etc. These
screen symbols help the neophyte execute various functions without typing multiple key
commands. The user simply selects the picture
of the task to be performed and presses Escape
or Return. However, in some cases the continual return to the icon menu can slow down the
writing process.

Imbedded command. <u>See</u> Embedded command.

Impact printer
A printer that uses its printing head to impact against a ribbon, transferring ink to the
paper. Dot-matrix printers are of the impact
variety, creating characters and graphics from
individual dots in a matrix or grid. Another
type of impact printer is the daisy wheel,
sometimes described as a die-impact printer.
Its characters are fully formed, like those of
a die, each of which impacts against the ribbon to produce letter-quality print indistinguishable from that of high-priced electronic

typewriters. <u>See</u> <u>also</u> Non-impact printer.

Incremental spacing. <u>See</u> Horizontal motion index.

Indentation
The number of spaces from the left line at which a paragraph begins. Various WPs have different default values for indenting paragraphs whenever the tab key is pressed. These default values can be changed. Some programs also provide for outdenting, a feature which brings the first line of a paragraph closer to the left margin while succeeding lines are indented. <u>See</u> <u>also</u> Hanging paragraph, Outdent.

Index
A WP application with the capability to mark particular words and phrases and to sort alphabetically key-word entries. Indexing is a complex task for a WP to perform. Therefore, few programs offer this feature. Samna Word III, for instance, compiles an index from a list of entries the user prepares. The program searches the text for these, sorts them alphabetically, and lists the page references for each. <u>See</u> <u>also</u> Alphabetical indexing.

Information
Data processed and converted into a more functional form so that the computer, the disk operating system, and the WP can manipulate it.

Initialized state
The default parameters of a printer when it is turned on. The initialized state often includes parameters for paper length and width, pitch, print head position, carriage return, etc.

Figure I.1   Initialized State
of a Typical Printer

Lines per inch	6
Characters per inch	10
Left margin	1
Right margin	72
Top margin	1
Bottom margin	66
Lines per page	66

Initializing a disk
Preparing a disk so that it can accept programs and/or text files from a WP. Apple computers use the term "initializing," while IBM
and similar systems apply the word "formatting." Both, however, perform the same operation. Initializing a disk destroys any information presently on it. Some WPs such as
AppleWriter II permit initializing from within
the program. This can be a useful feature,
especially when a document is ready to be
saved and no prepared disks are available. See
also Format.

Ink jet printer
A non-impact printer that sprays microscopic
spots of ink onto paper to form characters.
Ink jet printers are much quieter than either
dot-matrix or daisy-wheel printers and about
equal in print quality to that of dot-matrix
machines. See also Printer.

Input
Data or information which is transferred from
an external source such as a disk drive into
the internal memory of a computer.

Input/Output
The exchange of data between a computer and a
peripheral device such as a disk drive, modem,

printer, etc.; also, between the user and the computer. An input/output system is one of the three essential parts of a computer, the other two being the central processing unit, or CPU, and the memory portion. The term input/output is sometimes written as "I/O." <u>See</u> <u>also</u> CPU, Memory, RAM, ROM.

Insert
To add text to a document on screen. Text can be inserted in two ways, often called insertion modes. As the user types in new material, current text moves to the right of the cursor or "wraps around" (word wrap) onto the next line. This procedure is sometimes called nondestructive insert mode, since it does not erase current text. In the second method, the new text overwrites the old, erasing it. This is known as destructive insert mode. Most WPs provide both methods, each controlled by the insert key. Some programs such as Applewriter II offer only Insert and not the overwrite mode. Insert is one of the key functions and advantages of word processing.

Figure I.2   Example of Nondestructive Insert

(before insert)

Several eyewitnesses confirm that Charlie Chaplin's outfit had its origin in his first film.

(after insert)

Several eyewitnesses, among them Chester Conklin and Minta Durfee, confirm that Charlie Chaplin's outfit had it origin in "Kid Auto Races," his first film.

Figure I.3   Example of Destructive Insert

> (before insert)
>
> It was Edison who remarked: "Genius
> is one percent inspiration and 99 per-
> cent perspiration."
>
> (after insert)
>
> It was Thomas Alva Edisond: "Genius
> is one percent inspiration and 99 per-
> cent perspiration."

Insert cursor
A term used by some WPs such as AppleWorks to
describe an editing procedure in which text is
inserted into a document while old text is
moved to the right. The insert cursor, in
relation to these programs, differs from the
overstrike cursor, which replaces current text
as new text is inserted. See also Insert.

Insert key
The key that turns the insert mode on and off.
With insert on, text can be entered without
deleting present text. With insert off, any
text which is entered prints over the current
text on screen. Virtually all WPs utilize the
insert key.

Insert line
A function of some WPs which permits the user
to enter one or more blank lines into a document on screen. The insert line is used to
provide space for text insertion without having the following line continuously move down.

Insert mode
A function that allows text to be entered into
a document on screen without erasing or writ-

ing over current text. When a WP is in insert mode, all current text is moved to the right of the cursor as new characters are entered. With the insert mode in the off position, current text is replaced by new entries.

Installation routine
A procedure necessary before special printer functions can operate with a particular WP. Many WPs provide a utility program in which the user follows a series of prompts concerning the capabilities of the printer to be used. The special functions usually include underlining, boldface, subscripts, and superscripts. Installations can very often handle data related to dozens of popular printers. These routines are relatively easy to perform, but some WPs require a procedure involving 13 pages of instructions. Without these routines, many of the above functions might not work with a specific WP program. WordStar, for example, does not utilize some advanced features of certain printers, such as microjustification with proportional spacing. NewWord, on the other hand, takes advantage of this feature as well as variable character width, alternate pitches within one line, etc.

Figure I.4   Sample Installation Routine

1. Turn computer on with CP/M disk in Drive A
2. Insert WP disk in Drive B
3. Type DIR B: Press Return
4. Type N
5. For choice of printer, type name of printer
6. Type L (for CP/M list device)
7. Type Y to confirm choice.

Instruction
An individual command from a computer program
such as a WP. Instructions may be assigned to
the computer, a disk drive, or a printer.

Figure I.5   Sample Instructions

```
              (to the computer)

    Control B       Mark a block of text
    Control M       Move a block of text
    Control R       Remove a block of text

              (to the disk drive)

    Control S    Save document as text file
    Control L    Load file to screen
    Control D    Delete file from disk

               (to printer)

    Control P       Print current document
    Control PS      Underline text
    Control PB      Print text in boldface
```

Integrated software
A program which contains other programs so
that they can be used simultaneously or data
can be transferred between them. For example,
AppleWorks contains a WP, a database, and a
spreadsheet. Information from one can be entered into another.

Intelligent error message
An on-screen statement prompting the user
about a mistake and a suggested correction.
MultiMate, for instance, uses intelligent
error messages when it tells the user to close
the drive door if it has been left open. Many

117

WPs provide a simple error message on screen without designating what the problem is.

Figure I.6   Two Types of Error Messages

```
        (error message)

        I/O ERROR

   (intelligent error messages)

     CLOSE DISK DRIVE DOOR
     PRINTER IS NOT ON
```

Interface
Communication between a computer and a peripheral such as a printer or between two computer systems.

Interface card
An electronic device designed to connect a computer and its peripherals with external sources of information. For example, some peripheral cards allow the computer to communicate with a printer, while others communicate with a modem.

Internal storage
Storage inside the computer, and controlled by the central processing unit. See also Computer memory, CPU, External memory.

Intra-word justification. See Microjustification.

Inverse video
The presentation of characters on screen in black on a light background. Inverse video, sometimes known as reverse video, is often used for special functions such as displaying

118

boldface, underlining, marking blocks of text for relocation, etc. It is also used in menu headings or titles. Some WPs utilize inverse video to differentiate between prompt questions and responses.

I/O error
An error message which refers to the inability of the system to read (input) or write (output) to a disk. I/O errors can result from the following: failure to close the disk drive door, use of a defective disk, running a disk drive without a disk inserted, or not turning on or warming up the hard disk drive. See also Intelligent error message.

J

Job
A designated set of tasks directed as a unit of work for a computer to execute.

Joining text files
The ability of a WP to add another file to a document in memory or to a document to be printed. Some WPs can join or link files from other sources such as those created on other WPs. Joining text files makes editing easier, since blocks can readily be moved from one part of a document to another. The procedure also facilitates printing by eliminating continual loading and other preparations. Some WPs automatically reformat the second file to conform to the document on screen. Files are linked in the order in which they are entered. Some WPs have certain restrictions concerning linking files. For instance, the number of files may depend on the number of characters in each file name. Some programs make a distinction between "appending files" and "joining files." PFS: Write, for example, uses "append" to join a file on disk to a document on screen, reserving the term "join" for linking a series of files to be printed. See also Appending files, Merge.

Jump feature
A function that allows the cursor to skip over text to different places in a document. Some jump features include moving the cursor to the beginning or the end of text, the previous or next page or screen, and the beginning or the end of a line or paragraph. Usually the more costly the WP, the more sophisticated the jump features. See also Cursor movement.

Figure J.1 Sample Menu of Jump Features

Control-N	Next page
Control-P	Previous page
Home key	Top of page
End key	Bottom of page
Control-Home	Beginning of document
Control-End	End of document

Justification. See Full justification, Center justification, Left justification, Right justification.

Justified text. See Full justification.

K

K
An abbreviation for kilobyte. "K" represents
the number 1,024, or approximately 1,000
bytes. Thus, a computer memory of 64K contains
over 64,000 bytes.

Key file
With some WPs, a storage file on disk for
holding macro commands or a key glossary. A
key file is used to call to screen for document insertion often-used multiple commands or
repeated phrases. See also Glossary, Key
procedure.

Figure K.1   Sample Key File

.HE   (for header)
.MT 6   (top margin lines)
.MB 4   (bottom margin lines)
.PN 1   (page number)

Key glossary. See Glossary.

Key procedure
The ability of a WP to save a series of key-

strokes, then call them back with one command. This feature is also known as Macro. See also Glossary.

See also Glossary.

Figure K.2   Sample Key Procedures
with Glossary Function

```
Ctrl G-w  =  word processing
Ctrl G-y  =  Yours truly,
Ctrl G-r  =  Random Access Memory
Ctrl G-n  =  (Your Name)
Ctrl G-a  =  (Your address)
```

Key repeat function. See Typematic.

Keyboard
The component of a computer system that communicates with the WP. The Apple keyboard resembles that of a conventional typewriter except for a few keys, such as Control and Delete. The IBM and similar keyboards are divided into three separate sections. To the left are 10 function keys (some keyboards place these keys horizontally along the top row); in the center are the letter keys similar to those of a standard typewriter; to the right is a numeric keypad. Most computer keyboards contain an escape key, a control key, arrow keys and a reset key. Other special keys include the backspace, number lock, insert, print screen, scroll lock, page up, page down, alternate, home and end keys.

There are two different configurations of the alphanumeric sections of a keyboard, the Qwerty and the Dvorak. The standard Qwerty system is the keyboard most typists and computer users are familiar with. Its name derives from the first six letters of the third row from the bottom. Another system, slowly gaining popularity, is the Dvorak, whose unique layout of characters reputedly allows the user to enter data at a much faster rate. See also Dvorak keyboard, Keyboard configuration, Qwerty keyboard.

Keyboard configuration
A method of defining the value of each key on the keyboard component of a word processor. Although virtually all systems come with a fixed or permanent configuration, some keyboards offer the user the option of the standard Qwerty or the allegedly more efficient Dvorak layout. Also, some WPs such as The Final Word and utility programs such as Smart-Key II allow the user to customize the conventional keyboard. Thus, the user can redefine any number of keys, usually in combination with the escape key, to perform special tasks. For example, the user can reconfigure the left arrow key to move text to the left (Esc <--), the "5" key to center text (Esc 5), and the right arrow key to move text to the right margin (Esc -->). Redefining keys can save keystrokes and make certain functions more accessible, since the user is determining which keys will represent a particular job. Finally, editing can be made more efficient by grouping keys together which perform related functions. See also Dvorak keyboard, Keyboard, Qwerty keyboard.

Keyboard entry. See Alphabetical indexing.

Keyboard glossary. See Key procedure.

Keyboard template
An overlay which is placed over the keyboard to help describe the various keyboard commands and their particular functions. Overlays are often supplied by the WP vendor or can be purchased by independent companies for the more popular programs.

Keyboarding
Entering information or data on a computer
keyboard or on a typewriter.

Keycap
A temporary replacement part provided by a WP
manufacturer which performs a specific command
as printed on the cap. Keycaps, although an
initial annoyance, allow WP commands to be
executed quickly, since the user does not have
to memorize them or resort to the documentation. WPs such as Word Juggler IIe, which utilize keycap commands, in effect create dedicated function keys, all labeled for easy use.

Kilobyte. See K.

L

Labeling a block. <u>See</u> Block copy.

Laser printer
A non-impact printer that uses bursts of
light, a laser beam, a rotating mirror, and a
series of lenses to produce letter-quality
print at high speeds. Some laser printers can
produce 300 characters per second, or eight
pages of print per minute. Besides their
speed, the printers run silently, since there
is no print head to hammer against a ribbon.
The one current drawback is the relatively
high price of laser printers; they cost anywhere from $3,000 to $10,000.

Layout
The visual presentation or format of the
printed page. Many WPs provide various features that can enhance and control the layout
of the final work. Some features that affect
layout include justification, indentation,
hanging paragraphs, bullets, page headers and
footers, etc. <u>See</u> <u>also</u> Format.

Left arrow key
A cursor control key used as a backspace function. On virtually all WPs, when the left arrow key is pressed, the cursor moves one space

to the left. With some programs, this key is combined with the control key to move the cursor one word to the left. Usually, moving the cursor to the left by means of the left arrow key is a nondestructive function; i.e., no characters in the path of the cursor are erased. See also Arrow key.

Left justification
Text that is even with the left margin. WPs provide left justification as their default value, which can be changed by the user to fit different needs. Text which has both left and right justification is known as full justification.

Figure L.1   Left Justification

"Annual income twenty pounds, annual expenditure nineteen nineteen six, result happiness. Annual income twenty pounds, annual expenditure twenty pounds ought and six, result misery."

David Copperfield

Figure L.2   Full Justification

"Annual   income   twenty   pounds,   annual expenditure nineteen nineteen six, result happiness. Annual income twenty pounds, annual expenditure twenty pounds ought and six, result misery."

David Copperfield

Letter quality
Printing resembling that produced by a typewriter. Letter-quality printers use a daisy wheel or thimble-type device with fully formed characters that are hammered against the inked ribbon and paper. This produces higher-quality printing than that of dot-matrix printers, known as correspondence quality. Letter-quality models are generally slower in operation and more expensive than correspondence-quality models. The average machine ranges in speed from about 18 characters per second (cps) to 55 cps, while dot-matrix printers produce copy anywhere from 40 (correspondence quality) to 180 (draft quality) cps. Some later models run at an even faster speed. Some dot-matrix printer manufacturers boast that their machines produce near-letter-quality print, but under close scrutiny, one can see the difference; at the present time there is no substitute for letter-quality print. See also Dot-matrix printer, Impact printer, Non-impact printer.

Library
A collection of programs or files, usually on a floppy or hard disk or on magnetic tape. See also Glossary.

Line delete
A function of many WPs whereby an entire line can be removed by one command. Some WPs provide the ability to restore the line if the user so desires. With other programs, the line is permanently erased. Also, some programs provide a sentence-delete feature in addition to line delete. This, however, is one of the luxuries of higher-priced programs. See also Vertical slide.

Figure L.3   Line Delete

```
                    (before)

    Costello: Who's on first?
    Costello: You know the fellow's name?
    Abbott: Yes.
    Costello: I mean the guy playing first.
    Abbott: Who.
    Costello: The first baseman.
    Abbott: Who.

                    (after)

    Costello: Who's on first?
    Abbott: Yes.
    Costello: I mean the guy playing first.
    Abbott: Who.
    Costello: The first baseman.
    Abbott: Who.
```

Line feed
A symbol placed at the end of each line,
usually noted on screen by a symbol placed in
the right margin at the end of a line. Some
printers and WPs require these symbols to
ensure proper spacing between lines.

Line field. See Line indicator.

Line graphics
A feature that permits the user to draw horizontal and vertical lines. Line graphics is a
useful function for creating charts, graphs,
etc. The alternative to this, the use of the
underline and the vertical bar, is both cum-
bersome and time-consuming.

Line indicator
The item on a status display or status line
that indicates the number of the line at the

top of the screen or the number of the line at which the cursor is placed. The line indicator, also called line field, is useful in determining how much space is left on the present page on screen. This is especially helpful in planning tables and graphs, which ordinarily must be printed in their entirety on one page. Line indicators can be found at the top or bottom of a display screen, depending on the individual WP.

Figure L.4   Line Indicator Status Line

```
+-----------------------------------------------+
|  _____  |
|                                               |
|   File: TEST   Page: 1  Line: 4   Column: 1   |
|  _____  |
|                                               |
|                                               |
|   _ (cursor)                                  |
|                                               |
+-----------------------------------------------+
```

Line-oriented editor
An editing procedure, now almost obsolete, that requires the entry of a carriage return at the end of each line. Most WPs today use its counterpart, the full-screen editor, that employs word wrap, a process that moves text automatically to the next line. See also Full-screen editor, Word wrap.

Line printer
A device that prints all characters of a line as a unit. Line printers are known more for their speed than for their quality.

Line spacing
The number of blank lines printed between text lines. Some WPs allow single-, double-, or triple-spacing. Other WPs offer either single-

130

spacing only or two options, single or double. A few programs provide more than triple-spacing. Line spacing can be controlled through printer codes if the WP does not offer the proper options. Some programs display the spacing selection on screen to remind the user of the mode and to show true page breaks. The latter is important when the user has to insert a chart or table into a document. If the spacing reflects the way the document will appear when it is printed, the user can determine if the full chart or table should be placed on the present page or moved to the following one. See also Half-line spacing, Double space, Vertical spacing.

Lines per page. See Page break, Page length.

Lines per screen
Refers to the number of lines available on the display screen for entering text. This number varies with each WP, depending upon how many lines are utilized for the ruler line, command line, permanent menus, etc. Although some programs display extensive menus on the top part of the screen, consuming many lines, these WPs usually provide a feature that allows the user to remove these utilities. Some people prefer an uncluttered screen in which they can review as much of a document as possible. The number of lines per screen available for use doesn't fluctuate much between WPs. They range from 20 (DisplayWrite and Personal Qwerty) to 25 (Spellbinder). See also Display screen.

Linking files. See Joining text files.

Load
To retrieve a file stored on a disk and place it into the computer memory, usually for editing or printing purposes. Loading a file may be accomplished in various ways, depending on

the individual WP. For instance, the command
Control L can be used, or with some programs,
a number or letter is selected from a menu of
options. Editing a file loaded in memory does
not alter the original file on disk unless the
new version is saved, in which case the old
file is written over by the revised one. This
function is sometimes called by another name.
PFS: Write, for instance, uses the term "get
document," which appears on screen along with
save and remove.

Lock
To protect a file from being overwritten or
deleted. Some WPs such as Applewriter II provide an option that permits the user to lock a
file. Such files are displayed with an asterisk preceding each name when the catalog is
listed on screen. A locked file, however, is
not protected if the disk is reformatted or
initialized. Files can be unlocked by a similar command from the same option menu that
locked the file. Some WPs use the terms "protect" and "unprotect." See also Unlock.

Logged disk
The default disk currently in use. Some WPs
such as WordStar and NewWord permit changing
the disk drive from within its program and
during editing. See also Change logged disk
drive, Default drive.

M

Machine language
The built-in language of a computer. Machine language is written in binary numbers, such as 1100011. Other languages include assembly language and high-level language (BASIC, COBOL, etc).

Macro. See Glossary, Key procedure.

Macro command
A method of customizing a program using single keystrokes. One control sequence can be designed to perform a combination of functions, or a task usually requiring a series of strokes. Many of the more sophisticated and more costly WPs permit the user to create a library of personal macros. See also Glossary, Key procedure.

Magnetic card
A plastic card used for storing information or data. Also known as mag card.

Magnetic tape
Tape containing a magnetic coating or surface on which data can be stored. Magnetic tape, which can store large amounts of information in contrast to floppy disks, is often used as

a backup storage system for hard disk drives.

Mail merge
A feature that permits one file of data to be inserted into another file containing a form letter. Mail merge usually integrates with certain WPs. Usually, the mail merge procedure consists of first setting up a form letter that contains special markings at places where information is to be inserted. This is sometimes called a template. Another file is then created with the data intended to be entered into the form letter. Some WPs include a mail merge program, while others offer it as an option. See also Mailing list, Template.

Mailing list
A feature of many top-of-the-line WPs that allows a list of names and addresses to be integrated with a form letter. The program extracts each name and address and places it into the letter while removing the old ones. See also Mail merge.

Main menu
A help menu that lists other menus as well as other important information concerning text editing. Some WPs such as Newscript open with a main menu, while others begin with an opening menu that leads into a main menu. A main menu ordinarily provides access to an editing menu, a print menu, a spelling checker, utility menus for installing or customizing printers, and other help menus. Some WPs provide a feature that allows the user to remove the main menu from the screen, thereby producing more lines per screen for editing a document. See also Opening menu, Submenu.

Figure M.1 Main Menu of AppleWorks

```
1. Add files to the Desktop
2. Work with one of the files on Desktop
3. Save Desktop files to disk
4. Remove files from the Desktop
5. Other activities
6. Quit
```

Figure M.2 Multimate's Main Menu

```
1) Edit an Old Document
2) Create a New Document
3) Print Document Utility
4) Printer Control Utilities
5) Merge Print Utility
6) Document Handling Utilities
7) Other Utilities
8) Spell Check a Document
9) Return to DOS

       DESIRED FUNCTION:  _

Enter the number of the function
        and press RETURN

Hold down Shift and press F1 for HELP
```

Manual page break. See Conditional page break,
Discretionary page break.

Margin
A parameter or border set by a WP beyond which
text cannot be entered. Virtually all WPs have
default values or permit the user to set values that affect the top, bottom, left, and
right margins. Screen-oriented WPs such as
PFS: Write display these margins so that the
user can see what the page will look like

before it is printed on paper. Other WPs such
as Applewriter II permit margins to be entered, but, except for left justification,
they are not visible on screen. Some programs
permit internal blocks of text to have different margins from the rest of the document,
simply by entering embedded dot commands or
multiple ruler lines. Left and right margins
are usually preset; these default values can
be changed to meet specific needs. See also
Dot command, Embedded command, Multiple
rulers.

Figure M.3   Left and Right Margins
on Ruler Line

```
                   (default settings)

   L------^------^------^------^------R

                   (new settings)

   L--^--------------------------^---R
```

Margin setting
An adjustment made within the WP program that
controls the size of the left, right, top, and
bottom margins. The typical WP provides a set
of default values for these parameters, e.g.,
LM = 10, RM = 65, TM = 6, BM = 6. Of course,
any one or all of these numbers can be
changed, depending on the particular requirements of the text. On most WPs, margins can be
set before or after text is entered. With some
programs, files that are appended to the document on screen conform to the margin settings
of that document. Margin settings normally
include headers and footers. See also Margin.

Marker
A symbol or character used to mark a part of a
document intended for saving, loading, moving,
or transferring. To perform one of these functions, the text has to be marked to distinguish that particular segment from the remainder of the text. For instance, with Apple-
Writer II, to save only a part of a document
to disk, a marker is placed at the end of the
segment that is to be saved. The marker the
user selects should be a character that is not
used elsewhere in the text, such as "^" or
"+." The cursor is then placed at the beginning of that passage. When Control S(ave) is
pressed, all the user has to do in response to
NAME: is type the new name along with the
marker (NEWNAME/^/).

Mass storage device
An instrument that can hold large amounts of
information. Some examples of mass storage
devices are the floppy disk, the hard disk,
and tape. See also Floppy disk, Hard disk,
Magnetic tape.

Master disk. See Program disk.

Math mode
A feature that allows the user to perform such
operations as addition, subtraction, multipli-
cation, division, and percentage calculations.
Programs such as Samna Word III permit the
transfer of mathematical results into the
text. Some models of WPs, such as Wordstar
2000, may have a math mode, while other models, such as WordStar 3.3, do not offer this
feature. Other WP programs that contain math
functions include Spellbinder 5.3 and Display-
Write 3.

Matrix printer. See Dot-matrix printer.

Megabyte
One million bytes. One megabyte is usually
written as 1MB. Soft disk drives are usually
measured in kilobytes (K), while hard disk
drives are measured in megabytes, some featur-
ing 10MB, others 20 MB, and so on. One megabyte equals 1,048 kilobytes (1,000K) or
1,048,576 bytes.

Memory. See Computer memory.

Memory-based WP
A WP that depends upon the amount of memory
available in the computer after taking into
account the WP program and other housekeeping
tasks. Therefore, a system that contains 128K
(kilobytes) of memory may only provide 55K of
usable memory for text. The length of a document written with memory-based WPs conse-
quently is limited by the size of the memory
available. Documents, however, can be divided
into chapters or other sections. Memory-based
WPs usually feature a linking function that
permits a chain of related files to be printed
as one long document. The counterpart to the
memory-based WP is the disk-based system. See
also Disk-based WP.

Memory-oriented WP
A WP that does not automatically save on-
screen text periodically. To save a current
document with memory-oriented WPs, the user
must type the save command. Because a document
may be lengthy and involve many hours of typing, those who have had experience with this
type of program recommend that the user save
the text every 20 or 30 minutes. This procedure will help avoid losing the entire work
in case of a power failure or other accident.

Menu

A list of options or functions available from a program. WPs generally provide two basic types of menus: main menus and submenus, the former usually appearing after the program is booted. Programs normally allow access to the main menu from other menus. Sometimes the main menu is referred to as the opening menu, although a few WPs make a clear distinction between these. Menus can provide information about cursor movement, editing functions such as Delete and Block Move, formatting, printing, loading and saving files, initializing disks, and installation procedures. For some of these more esoteric chores, such as installing a printer to operate compatibly with a WP, a submenu permits the user to select the proper machine. The screen then gives a series of instructions and prompts. Probably one of the most useful series of menus, especially for the novice, is the help menu. See also Help menu, Main menu, Opening menu.

Figure M.4   Example of a General Menu

```
1. EDIT              5. DISPLAY DIRECTORY

2. PRINT             6. INSTALL

3. CHECK SPELLING    7. GET/SAVE/REMOVE

4. MAIL MERGE        8. EXIT TO DOS

           9. HELP

      Select Number _ and

     Press Escape or Return
```

Figure M.5   A Specific Menu

```
┌─────────────────────────────────────────────┐
│                                               │
│           PRINTER SELECTION MENU              │
│                                               │
│    1. Centronics          5. Epson            │
│                                               │
│    2. Okidata             6. Diablo           │
│                                               │
│    3. NEC Spinwriter      7. C. Itoh          │
│                                               │
│    4. Anadex              8. Other            │
│                                               │
│       FOR INSTALLATION PROCEDURES,            │
│     SELECT NUMBER _ and PRESS RETURN          │
│                                               │
└─────────────────────────────────────────────┘
```

Menu-driven WP
A WP that operates mainly by selections and
options made available by various menus. Menu-
driven WPs are easier to use, requiring less
time to memorize numerous commands and function keys. However, they can slow down the
operation of a WP, since the user must wait
for each menu or submenu to appear on screen.
Menu-driven programs usually operate by the
selection of a particular function, such as
Edit, Print, or Save. After the initial selection is made, a submenu or list of subfunctions appears and one of these is chosen. The
counterpart to the menu-driven WP is the command-driven WP, which requires pressing the
control, alternate, or shift key in combination with others to perform various functions.
For instance, to save a document onto a disk
using a menu-driven WP, the user must first
locate the proper menu and then press a number
or letter. To perform the same function with
a command-driven WP, the user simply presses a
few keys such as Control and S (for "Save").
Some WPs such as Cut & Paste, WordStar, Word
Perfect, DiplayWrite, and Volkswriter offer
both methods. See also Command-driven WP.

140

Figure M.6   Comparison of
Menu- and Command-driven WPs

MENU-DRIVEN	COMMAND-DRIVEN
1. LOAD	Control L
2. SAVE	Control S
3. PRINT	Control P
4. CENTER TEXT	Control C
5. JUSTIFY TEXT	Control J
6. EXIT TO DOS	Control E

Merge
To enter data or information into a document
in memory. Many WPs offer a merge feature,
especially one involving mailing and addres-
sing functions. Merging can entail multiple
steps. The document may have to be "marked" as
to where the additional data is to appear; an
electronic form may have to be completed; the
file name may have to be typed in; and the new
information may have to be "told" whether it
is to be justified or centered. Merge is one
of the many practical and often-used tools
that prove the superiority of word processing
over conventional typing. See also Appending
files, Block move, Document assembly, Joining
text files.

Figure M.7   Merging Data from
Two Documents

```
        (main document before merge)

|name|
|address|

Dear |last name|

Thank you for purchasing our |product|.
We know it will give you many years of
trouble-free service.

        (same document after merge)

Mr. Hiram Jones
123 Central Road
New City, CA   31277

Dear Mr. Jones:

Thank you for purchasing our Utopian
One-Pull Lawn Mower. We know it will
give you many years of trouble-free
service.
```

Microcomputer
A highly integrated, small computer system
based upon a CPU (central processing unit) or
microprocessor, input/output interfaces and
memory, and a power supply. Microcomputers
perform the same input, processing, storage,
and output functions as larger computers do.
Personal computers are considered microcomputers.

Micro-floppy disk
A 3 1/2-inch disk capable of storing the same
amount of data as a 5 1/4-inch floppy disk.
See also Floppy disk.

Microjustification
A feature of some WPs that combines true proportional spacing with full justification.
Microjustification allots a different unit of
space for characters of different width so
that the final printing gives the appearance
of typesetting. Full justification as offered
by most WPs inserts additional spaces between
words so that a line of text extends from the
left to the right margins. With microjustification the spacing between characters and
words allows for more accuracy and naturalness
by eliminating much of the superfluous white
space on each line. This feature usually requires the use of a daisy wheel printer. Some
owners of WPs use the terms "proportional
spacing" and "microjustification" interchangeably. The former term, in its strictest
meaning, does not imply full justification, as
does the latter. See also Proportional spacing, True proportional spacing.

Microprocessor. See CPU.

Microspace
A fraction of the standard width assigned by a
printer to each character. Most printers allot
the same width to a character regardless of
that character's width. An "i," for instance,
is treated the same as a "w" or an "m." Microspace incrementation varies the size of
each space attributed to a character during
justification. See also Microjustification,
Proportional spacing.

Mnemonic command
A keyboard or control command that starts with
the first letter of the function. It is much
easier for a user to remember Control L for
Load and Control S for Save than to have to
recall a non-mnemonic character. The more
mnemonic commands a WP employs, the more user-

friendly it is for the novice as well as the experienced user.

Mode
A method of operation. In WPs, for example, the insert mode permits the user to add text to a document on screen without overwriting or deleting current text. All characters move to the right and to the next line as new material is typed in. Also, there are various modes of justification, such as left, center, right, and full justify. See also Background mode, Foreground mode.

Modem
A device that permits data or information to be transmitted over telephone lines. The word "modem" is an acronym for modulate/demodulate. A modem converts digital information into analog format and vice versa. Modem connections can be either internal or external. The speed of a modem is measured by its baud rating, with the two most popular models rated at 300 and 1200 baud. See also Baud rate.

Monitor
The component of a computer system that resembles a television screen and allows the user to create and edit documents. There are monochrome and color monitors. Color monitors come in either video or RGB (red, green, blue) models, the latter producing better definition. A monochrome monitor or computer display device consists of three basic components. The electronic gun transmits a beam of electrons to a screen. The yoke focuses the beam at one point on the screen. The screen, which contains a phosphor coating, glows when hit by the electrons. A monochrome monitor is usually recommended for use with WP programs since it provides better resolution than many color displays. See also Color monitor, Display.

Mouse

An external device connected to the computer to operate the cursor. The cursor can be moved by the mouse to place a pointer over a particular function. When one of the buttons on the mouse is pushed, that function is activated. Some WPs utilize the mouse to make the program easier for beginners. The mouse can open, enlarge, decrease, and close windows much more easily than menus can. Some who are experienced with WPs believe the use of this device slows them down because one hand must leave the keyboard to control the buttons on the mouse. See also Window.

Move

To position the cursor or text. Depending upon the sophistication of the WP, the cursor can be moved one character, word, sentence, line, or page at a time; or it can be moved to the beginning or end of the document on screen. The more flexible the cursor movement, the easier it is to edit a document. Moving text is another useful feature. Blocks of text can be moved to other parts of a document or to a disk for later use.

Multi-line header/footer

The ability of a WP to provide more than one line for a heading or for the bottom of a page. Many WPs allow the user to create headers and footers, but usually limit these to a single line of text. Although admittedly it is a minor feature, the multi-line header or footer offers a greater range of possibilities.

Multilingual word processor

A system that can keyboard, store, and print files in different languages.

Multiple copies

The ability of a WP to direct the printer to produce more than one copy of a document. PFS: Write, for example, has an option within its print menu that asks the user to select the number of copies he or she wishes. All the user has to do is select a number. Some printer buffers that are sold as accessories can reproduce more than 250 copies through the use of a software command.

Multiple disk drives

A computer system with more than one disk drive, usually one for the program disk (Drive 1 or A) and the other for the data disk (Drive 2 or B). Some WPs require that the drive with the data or text disk be specified before a file is printed. Other WPs permit the user to choose either drive. The program will then print text files whose names are entered from both drives. With Apple II machines using the AppleWriter II program, for instance, the drive must be stated before loading or saving a file. Otherwise the program resorts to the default drive (the one last used). Therefore, after booting from Drive 1 and creating a document, the user must type the number of the second drive before attempting to save a document.

Figure M.8   Using AppleWriter II
with Multiple Drives

Save: Newfile,d2

Load: Glossary,d1

Delete: Newfile,d2

Multiple-file editing

The ability of a WP to permit the user to edit
more than one file simultaneously. Multiple
file editing is usually accomplished by having
two or more documents or parts of documents
present on the display screen at the same
time. Some WP programs allow more than one
file to appear on the screen, but provide no
means of editing both. See also Boilerplating,
Split screen.

Figure M.9   Example of a Multiple-File Screen

> When two files appear on the screen
> at the same time, they are usually dis-
> played horizontally as in this example.
> The viewer can then compare the text of
> each....
>
> ---
>
> Sometimes this procedure is called
> a split-screen. Some programs allow the
> user to move text from one part to the
> other. This can be a very useful feature
> when editing is required...

Multiple function key

A function key that is assigned more than one
task by a WP. Some WPs such as Samna Word III
designate a number of jobs to some of the
function and special function keys. This program, for instance, defines F5 on the IBM and
similar keyboards as Select and has it handle
numerous tasks.

Figure M.10   Example of a
Multiple Function Key

Key or Keys	Function
F1	Main menu
Alt F1	Previous page
Control F1	End of line
Shift F1	End of paragraph

Multiple rulers

A WP's use of several ruler lines within the
same document. A ruler provides information
such as tab stops and left and right margins.
The user may wish to use several rulers within
the same text when, for example, a long quota-
tion needs to be set off from the rest of the
document or a poem excerpt is included. Some
WPs accomplish this by the use of embedded
commands, which requires turning on the new
rulers as they are encountered. Other WPs such
as NewWord automatically alter the ruler line
each time it comes across one during vertical
scrolling. Although multiple rulers are installed in the document to assist the user,
they do not appear in print. Rules are sometimes called format lines. See also Ruler
line.

Figure M.11   Using Multiple Ruler Lines

```
              (document default line)

|-----^------------------------------|


     Poet John Donne's famous Meditation
XVII may be written in prose, but it
contains much that is poetic:

              (second ruler line)

  L----^--------------------------R


     Any man's death diminishes me
because I am involved in mankind,
and therefore never send to know
for whom the bell tolls; it tolls
for thee.
```

Multiple text columns. See Column mode.

Multiprogramming
Executing more than one program simultaneously
by a computer.

N

Near-letter-quality
A term describing print produced by a dot-matrix printer which uses various methods to achieve a higher-quality print than the standard correspondence quality produced by this type of machine. Near letter-quality, or NLQ as it is sometimes called, may be produced by increasing the number of print head wires from nine to 18 or 24. The additional wires create a more solid-looking character than one made with the conventional nine dots. Another method of producing NLQ is to have the print head strike each character a second time, with the second strike slightly moved so that the dot density appears increased. No matter how sophisticated or expensive the dot-matrix printer is, and regardless of the techniques employed to create better-quality type, the machines have not been able to equal the letter-quality print of the daisy wheel printer. The various qualities of print from a dot-matrix machine are, in ascending order, draft, enhanced, correspondence, and near-letter-quality. Many machines, however, especially models in the lower and medium price range, offer only the first three modes. See also Dot-matrix printer, Letter quality.

Nested indentation
A procedure in which each additional text
entry is moved to the left of the previous
one. The creation of outlines, for instance,
requires that each subtopic be indented an
additional number of spaces. Nested indentations are also useful in preparing lists. WPs
such as HomeWord accomplish this task with
indented point option. See also Nested paragraph.

Figure N.1   Example of Nested Indentation

```
A. Printers for Word Processors
   I. Dot-Matrix Printers
      a. Low-priced models
      b. Medium-range models
      c. Top-of-the-line models
         1. With near letter-quality
         2. With correspondence quality
  II. Daisy Wheel Printers
B. Printers for Spreadsheets
```

Nested menu
A list of instructions, options, or commands
available to the user once it is invoked to
the screen. Some WPs provide all their functions through multiple control keys which have
to be memorized if the program is to be operated efficiently. Other WPs offer these same
functions through a single keystroke once the
proper nested menu is called to the screen.
This saves all the memorization, but takes
time, as the user leaves the edit mode and
programs each menu to come and go from the
display screen. To save a document using a
WP's control keys, for example, may require
pressing an arcane Control-K-D or Control-O-S.
With a program employing nested menus, all the
user need do is find the appropriate menu and

press S(ave) or another letter or number listed on that menu.

Nested paragraph
A format tool of a WP used to indent individual paragraphs so that they are set within their own margins. Nested paragraphs are important in quoting passages, typing poems, and inserting tables and charts. These blocks of text need to be set off from the remainder of the document, exempt from its margins, and indented beyond the last passage. Nested paragraphs are also useful in sentence and paragraph outlining. See also Nested indentation.

Nesting
A term used to describe the placement of instructions or commands into a program or part of one. For example, in a mail merge program, which often is a part of a WP program, it is possible to insert or "nest" a variety of conditions so that only certain clients' names and addresses receive a particular letter. Conversely, nesting can help to omit a list of customers from a mailing, e.g., removing their names from a list targeted at those who are delinquent in their bills. See also Mail merge, Merge.

Network
A system of linking more than one communicating terminal or computer through electronic transmission.

No-file level
A WP mode such as an opening-menu presentation in which no file is being edited. The list of options or commands shown on screen can vary greatly and may include printing choices, other menu options, subprograms such as a spelling checker or mail merge, etc. The no-file level allows several operations to be performed, including changing the default

152

drive, deleting or renaming a file, etc. This
level also allows, with some WPs, a choice of
the document or non-document mode. See also
Non-document mode.

Figure N.2   Example of a No-File Level
             Screen Display

```
                  Opening Menu

     C- Change Disk Drive    S- Spell Check

     F- File Directory       R- Rename a File

     L- Load a File          D- Delete a File

     M- Mail Merge           P- Print a File
```

Non-break space. See Hard space.

Non-destructive backspace
A key which, when used in conjunction with
particular WPs, moves the cursor to the left
without altering the present text on screen.
The left-arrow key normally functions as a
non-destructive backspace key in such WPs as
Applewriter II, MultiMate, PFS: Write, and
WordStar. In fact, WordStar employs the backspace key as an alternative non-destructive
backspace. Other WPs like NewWord utilize the
left-arrow key as a destructive backspace. See
also Backspace.

Non-document mode
A method of operation which permits a WP program to function like a typewriter. The non-
document mode is useful for typing random
envelopes without having to program complex WP
formats. It can also be used for typing in
programs. This mode is a more direct text

entry procedure than its counterpart, the document mode, which is the primary operating method of virtually all WPs.

Non-impact printer

A printer that produces computer-generated documents under quieter conditions with greater mechanical reliability than an impact printer such as a dot-matrix or daisy-wheel machine. Non-impact printing includes thermal, electrosensitive, and ink-jet technologies. Thermal and electrosensitive, or electrostatic, printers require special paper onto which characters are printed by a special "burning" process. These printers are generally more costly than other types. Ink-jet technology utilizes a spraying technique and can produce colored or black characters or graphics. See also Electrostatic printer, Impact printer, Ink jet printer.

Nonprintable character

A character reserved by the WP program for a particular purpose when used as a special function key. Nonprintable characters often control printer functions. When a character is utilized in this fashion, it may not be printable. MultiMate, for example, uses a musical note as a symbol to designate a carriage return or the end of a paragraph.

Normal intensity

The adjustment of the contrast and brightness controls of a display monitor so that text and graphics on the screen appear comfortably readable to the user, while those portions in bright intensity seem highlighted. Some WPs utilize both bright and normal intensities in their menus to distinguish between headings and subheadings or to emphasize the user's responses to options or selections. Wordproof, for example, uses normal intensity for text entry, but with its synonym program, it highlights each word for emphasis. This text editor also uses both intensities in its command line on the bottom of the screen, again to point out to the user which commands are available. To take full advantage of these two intensities, the user may have to readjust the contrast and brightness controls. See also Bright intensity, Highlighting.

Number of copies. See Multiple copies.

Number of lines per page. See Page break, Page length.

Numeric keypad
The set of number keys usually found to the right of the conventional typewriter keyboard of a computer. The numeric keypad serves a dual role. When the number lock key is pressed, the numeric keypad operates like a calculator for entering figures in a spreadsheet or other program. When it is not activated, the keys are used to move the cursor in different directions, to display previous and following screens, to send the cursor to the beginning or end of the document, etc.

O

Object text. <u>See</u> Text object.

OCR. <u>See</u> Optical character reader.

Off-line
A peripheral device, such as a typewriter-printer, that operates independently of the central processing unit of a computer.

On-line
Any device connected directly to a computer. Some on-line items may be a disk drive, a modem, a printer, etc. <u>See</u> <u>also</u> Disk drive, Modem.

On-line help
Assistance to the user of a modem which is in operation. On-line help consists of typing a command to request either generalized or specific instructions. Typing HELP MAIL, for instance, will not get you into the electronic mail program, but it will show you how to enter the service. On-line help most often pertains to various options within a given program.

Figure 0.1   Examples of Commands
for On-Line Help

```
>HELP MAIL

>HELP SERVICES

>HELP COMMANDS

>HELP MANUAL
```

On-screen formatting
The ability of a WP to display on screen how
the printed page will look. WPs vary in their
ability to do this. Those that use embedded
commands to produce underlining or boldface,
for example, can only approximate the appearance of the printed document. Other programs
display these features in reverse video, so
the document is closer in appearance to the
printed page. The more sophisticated WPs,
however, provide actual underlining, boldface
(bright intensity), and italics on screen.

Figure 0.2   Example of On-Screen Formatting
without Embedded Commands

This text will appear on the
printed page exactly as it has been
typed on the screen. The underlining
appears on screen as actual underlining.

157

Figure 0.3   Example of On-Screen Formatting
with Embedded Commands

> This text contains embedded com-
> mands and will look slightly different
> on screen from the way it will appear on
> paper, especially the ^Uunderlining^U
> and ^Iitalics^I features.

On-screen help

A method of providing assistance to the user
by using the display screen in place of printed documentation. A WP can offer on-screen
help in various ways. A group of control key
functions or function keys with their uses may
appear on the bottom line of the screen. Some
programs provide help functions in the upper
region of the screen. These methods of help
are known as "continuous." The most frequent
and popular approach is the use of help
screens. This technique of help is called "on
demand." These screens can offer very general
information or extremely detailed lists of
commands and instructions, including editing
commands, formatting information, and printing
functions. On-screen help saves time by cir-
cumventing documentation, but it slows down
the WP as it waits for each screen to appear
and leave.

Figure 0.4   On-Screen Help
with Function Keys

F1- DISPLAY HELP	F2- DISPLAY SEARCH
F3- BEGIN SEARCH	F4- SPELL CHECK
F5- TABS	F6- INSERT LINE
F7- ERASE LINE	F8- DISPLAY COMMANDS
F9- BOLDFACE	F10- UNDERLINE

158

Figure 0.5   On-Screen Help with Control Keys

```
                    Cursor Movement

    Ctrl-E  Up 1 line      Ctrl-X  Down a line

    Ctrl-S  Char left      Ctrl-D  Char right

    Ctrl-A  Word left      Ctrl-F  Word right
```

Opening menu. See Main menu.

Operating system
That part of a computer which is divided into
ROM and RAM. The former, containing permanent
internal routine programs, activates various
functions such as the disk drive. The latter,
the computer's main memory and the major part
of most operating systems, usually gets its
information from a disk or from the keyboard.
RAM is often called volatile, since data entered into it are lost when the power is
turned off, unlike that of ROM. Some popular
operating systems, which are disk-based, include Apple's DOS and PRODOS, IBM's PC DOS, MS
DOS, TRSDOS, and CP/M, used by many different
computer systems. Operating systems are usually not compatible with each other, except when
they are specifically designed for this purpose, such as PC DOS and MS DOS. See also
CP/M, DOS, RAM, ROM.

Optical character reader (OCR)
An electronic device capable of recognizing
characters optically and transmitting them to
the screen and computer memory without their
having to be typed in manually. When interfaced with a computer, the OCR scans pages of
text, converting them into digital data which
can be handled by software. Although these

scanning systems are many times faster than any typist, most are limited by the number of fonts they can "read." The cost of an OCR varies greatly, ranging from approximately $500 to over $100,000.

Options menu
A menu or submenu which provides a list of functions from which the user may select. For instance, a print options menu usually includes such items as page length, left and right margins, top and bottom margins, number of lines per page, number of spaces between lines, header and footer, starting page number, etc. See also Main menu, Menu, Submenu.

Figure 0.6   Sample Options Menu

```
    1-   FIND TEXT IN FILE
    2-   FIND AND REPLACE
    3-   FIND MISSPELLING
    4-   FIND, REPLACE AND IGNORE CASE
    5-   RETURN TO EDIT MODE


         Select a Number
     and Press Return or Enter _
```

Orphan
A page of text that begins with the last line of a paragraph. Documents that have orphans are awkward in appearance. To improve the look of the page, some WPs permit the user to program documents so that the "orphan" line is printed along with its paragraph on the pre- vious page. "Orphans" are usually mentioned in combination with "widows." See also Widow.

Figure 0.7 Example of an Orphan

```
          (top of page)

of the results.
     The causes, however, are another
issue that must be dealt with. In fact,
these may affect every other aspect of
the problem.
```

Outdent
To place text past the left margin setting.
Some WPs such as Applewriter II provide this
feature through the use of negative embedded
command numbers. For example, the insertion of
a minus sign within a dot command causes text
to move to the left column a given number of
spaces (.PM-6 outdents the next line six
spaces left of the ordinary paragraph margin).
Outdenting can be a useful feature in outlining, setting certain paragraph formats,
etc. See also Indentation, Hanging paragraph.

Figure 0.8   Example of Outdenting

```
       (with normal margins)

     1. WPs should provide the necessary
     features for the tasks they will
     perform.

       (with outdenting)

  1. WPs should provide the necessary
     features for the tasks they will
     perform.
```

Outlining
A feature of some WPs which automatically

numbers and indents outline formats of multiple levels. Ordinarily, only the more costly
and sophisticated WP programs provide this
feature. There are three standards utilized in
outlining: Arabic, Roman (the most popular),
and Multi-level.

Figure 0.9   Three Types of Outlines

Arabic	Roman	Multi-level
1.	I.	1.
a.	A.	1.1
(1)	1.	1.1.1.
(a)	a.	1.1.1.1.

Overflow buffer
A method employed by some WPs to protect a-
gainst the loss of text when there are more
lines of text than can fit on the present
page. Additional lines of text are often added
during editing, but some WPs will not permit
these lines to be added to the current page
limit. Excess lines, therefore, are stored in
the overflow buffer. Each buffer can accommodate a certain number of lines. For instance,
one WP may store 80 lines of text. If this
limit is exceeded, loss of text can occur.
Usually, a notice appears on a part of the
screen when there is text stored in the buffer. See also Block buffer, Print buffer, Text
Buffer.

Overlay. <u>See</u> Shadow print.

Overprinting
Programming the WP so that the printer prints over the same line. This feature is used to display characters or words that have been stricken out of a document without deleting the text. Overprinting is sometimes required in official documents to show what has been deleted from the original. This feature is also known as zero line spacing.

Figure 0.10   Example of Overprinting

This is an example of ~~overpinting~~ overprinting. It displays the ~~deleeted~~ deleted words as well as the correctly spelled versions.

Overstrike
A WP mode in which new text replaces the existing text at the point of the cursor. Overstrike mode differs from insert mode which pushes existing text to the right to make room for the new material. Most WPs allow the user to switch back and forth between the two modes. Also called overtype, typeover, etc.

Overstrike cursor. <u>See</u> Insert cursor.

Overtype. <u>See</u> Insert.

P

Page
A general term used by many WPs to describe a screen filled with text, information, etc. The term "page" need not conform to a conventional page of printed text (66 lines for an 8 1/2 X 11-inch sheet of paper). With page-oriented WPs, a screen page refers to the parameters of a particular WP.

Figure P.1   Sample Menu with Page Options

Page Length	66	Lines per Page	55
Left Margin	0	Right Margin	65

Use Tab to Change Default
and Press Enter or Return

Page break
A predetermined point at which a WP program ends one page of a document and begins a new one. This location is sometimes called the default page break and usually is set at 66 lines. Virtually all WPs have a default set-

ting of six lines per inch. With standard
sheets of paper (8 1/2 X 11 inches), that
equals 66 lines per page. This does not equal
66 lines of text, however, since some lines at
the top and bottom of the page are reserved
for margins, leaving between 54 to 58 lines of
printed text. Page breaks may be changed on
most WP programs to accommodate special formatting needs. Some programs offer both automatic and manual page breaks. See also Conditional page break.

Page deletion

The removal of a page on disk. This function
is restricted to page-oriented WPs. To delete
a page, the name and number of the page must
usually be designated.

Page-down key

A function key used in conjunction with many
WPs to scroll down to the next screen of text
or to the next page if the program is page-
oriented. See also Page-up key.

Page length

A command option that permits setting a parameter for the number of text lines to be
printed per page. This number is usually
stored on the disk with each text file that is
saved. Before printing, the number of lines to
be printed can be changed by entering a new
figure. Depending upon the WP, page length
usually appears within a submenu called page
format, print options, print menu, etc. Page
length, also referred to as printed lines per
page, differs from paper length, which refers
to text lines as well as top and bottom margins. See also Paper length, Printed lines per
page.

Figure P.2 Page Length within a Page Menu

Left Margin	10	Page Length	55
Right Margin	70	Paper Length	66
Top Margin	6	Page Number	1
Bottom Margin	5	Line Spacing	1

Page number placement
The position of the page number on each page.
Some WP programs simply place the number,
centered, on the bottom of each page. Other
programs allow a choice, such as to the right,
center, etc. The more important function, to
some users, is alternating odd and even numbers on the right and left sides of consecutive pages for copy that is to be submitted
for photocopying. See also Alternate page
numbers.

Page numbering
The placing of numerals on each page of text
so that they automatically progress by one
throughout the document. Many WPs use the
footer function for this purpose, although the
header may also be employed. Any starting
number can be entered on the first page. Some
WPs such as PFS: Write permit the user to
enter Page 1 or Page A-1, where the program
reads only the number portion of the entry and
treats it as a page number.

Page-oriented WP
A description of a WP that organizes a working
document on screen into individual pages,
displaying only one page at a time. Since each
page acts as a separate entity, this may be
difficult for users unfamiliar with this approach. They cannot see what has gone before

unless they recall that page to the screen.
Page-oriented WPs, such as MultiMate, Display-
Write, and OfficeWriter nevertheless have pow-
erful features, some approaching the sophisti-
cation of dedicated WPs. See also Dedicated
WP, Document-oriented WP.

Page-up key
A function key that allows the user to examine
previous text by scrolling back one screen or
page at a time. The page-up key is usually
located on the number keypad, along with the
page-down key. See also Page-down key.

Pagination
A procedure for dividing multi-page documents
into individual pages by inserting page
breaks. See also Conditional page break, Page
break.

Paper feed device
A method of supplying paper to a printer.
There are two different devices used to feed
paper. The tractor feeder handles fanfold,
continuous-form paper that has perforations at
both ends. The most popular fanfold paper
measures 9 1/2 X 11 inches. When the edges
containing the perforations are removed and
the pages are separated, each page measures
8 1/2 X 11. The second device, the sheet
feeder, or cut-sheet feeder, automatically
supplies single sheets of paper to the printer. Some printers, such as the Okidata, have a
built-in tractor feeder.

Paper length
The entire length of a page, including the top
and bottom margins. Most WPs set the default
length at 66 for use with standard sheets of
paper. Paper length should not be confused
with page length or "printed lines per page,"
whose default setting usually ranges from 54
to 58. If other than 8 1/2 x 11-inch paper is

used, the default values for paper length must be readjusted. <u>See</u> <u>also</u> Page length, Printed lines per page.

Paragraph indentation. <u>See</u> Indentation, Outdent.

Paragraph reformatting
Realigning a paragraph of text on screen to its original parameters, especially after editing. On certain WPs such as WordStar 3.3, deleting or adding text causes blank spaces to appear within lines or characters to overrun a line. To align the paragraph to its original format, it must be reformatted. Other WPs such as WordStar 2000 and Applewriter II perform this task automatically.

Figure P.3   Paragraph Reformatting

(original text)

The Arabian riding camel, a
swift, domestic species not
found in the wild, is known
as the dromedary.

(additions to text)

The Arabian (one-humped) riding camel,
a swift, domestic species not
found in the wild, is known as
the dromedary.

(after reformatting)

The Arabian (one-humped) riding camel, a swift, domestic
species not found in the wild,
is known as the dromedary.

Paragraph tab
A text indentation function that temporarily alters the left margin to a tab stop and aligns all the following typewritten lines under the tabulation setting. This is useful for indenting lines of text quoted from other sources and set off from the remainder of the text in the document and footnoted, and in outlining.

Paragraphing
The method or methods a WP uses to begin or mark a new paragraph. Some of the ways WPs perform this function include the use of tabs, control keystrokes, the return key, or manual spaces. Different WPs mark paragraphs differently. WordStar, for instance, uses a "smaller than" symbol (<) at the end of a line to the right of the paragraph. See also Line-ending marker.

Parameter
A value necessary before a WP program can perform a particular operation. WPs often provide default parameters to handle such functions as left and right margins, tabs, lines per page, etc. These parameters can be altered to fit specific needs. See also Default parameter.

Parity
An error-detection procedure concerning data that are transmitted between a computer and a peripheral device such as a printer, disk drive, etc.

Partial printing
A WP feature that permits the user to produce a hard copy from a specified portion of the document on screen. Text Wizard, for example, uses the cursor, which can be placed anywhere;

all text below it will be printed. Other WPs
use different procedures. Some ask for a specific page number or series of pages; other
programs require that you mark the portion to
be printed, save it on disk under a new file
name, then load it for printing.

Password security
A code placed on a data disk through a WP to
ensure the privacy of the files stored on the
magnetic medium. Some WPs such as NBI provide
password security as one of their features.

Pathname
A series of file names divided by slashes and
displaying the full path from the directory to
the file that a WP must follow to locate a
particular file. Pathnames are important when
working with subdirectories. In the following
example, "A" represents the disk drive,
"Book," the pathname, "WP," the subdirectory,
and "RPT.," the text file.

Figure P.4   Pathname Sample

A:\BOOK\WP\RPT1.DOC

A:\BOOK\WP\RPT2.DOC

Pause
The ability of a printer to stop printing
temporarily when it receives a top-of-form
command. The message, which translates as "new
page," requires that the printer go into a
pause mode while a new sheet of paper is being
fed. Many WPs offer a pause feature that controls the printer. With these programs, Pause
halts the machine temporarily and, when reac-
tivated, continues from the point at which it
stopped. Pause differs from the stop function,

which is a permanent command in which the
printer returns to the start of the document
when printing is resumed.

Peripheral
A device designed to communicate with a computer. Modems, printers, keyboards, disk drives,
monitors, or other similar devices are considered peripherals.

Peripheral card. See Card.

Personal computer
A low-cost, compact computer made for an individual user, which can operate independently
of a large or mainframe computer. Personal
computers may be sold as separate components
with the display monitor, disk drives, and
accessory cables as optionals or as "packages"
that include the above peripherals. Some personal computer manufacturers offer "bundled"
software to get the user started. These programs often include a WP, a database, and/or a
spreadsheet. See also Computer.

Personal dictionary. See Custom dictionary.

Phrase search
A feature of certain WPs that locates a string
of words separated by blank spaces. If, for
example, the word "the" was the object of a
search, the program would also point out
"then," "there," "lathe," and all other occurrences in which the string "the" appears. If,
however, the target word included a blank
space (" the "), the search would be more
restrictive. In phrase searches, blank spaces
are automatically added before and after the
string of words. Words like "then" and "lathe"
would not be counted as occurrences of the
string "the." See also Search and replace.

PI. <u>See</u> Vertical motion index.

Pica
A character pitch with a width of 10 characters per inch, or cpi. Most printers, whether dot-matrix or daisy wheel, use pica as their default pitch. Other pitches include elite (12 cpi) and compressed or condensed (15 or 17 cpi).

Pitch
The number of characters per inch to be printed. The larger the number, the smaller the size of the print. Some WPs support multiple print pitches from five to 17 characters per inch, or cpi. Two of the most popular pitches are pica (10 cpi) and elite (12 cpi). Dot-matrix printers usually feature variable pitch ranging from 10 to 17 cpi as well as double width, etc. Daisy wheel models provide variable pitches, depending upon the print wheel that is currently installed.

Pixel
A screen element used as a unit of measurement. A pixel is the smallest single element addressable by the computer. The more pixels present on screen, the better the resolution or definition. Pixel is an acronym for picture element.

Platen width
The distance a print head travels from the extreme left margin to the extreme right. Some less costly printers supply a platen width sufficient for standard-size paper (8 1/2 X 11 or 8 1/2 X 14 inches), but not capable of handling legal envelopes or spreadsheets.

Pointer. <u>See</u> Type position pointer.

Pop-up menu. <u>See</u> Pull-down menu.

Previewing
A function of some WPs that shows by means of
a preview screen how the text will look when
it is printed on paper. These WPs do not
feature screen-oriented print. Some of these
programs, such as HomeWord, display a window
on the screen in the lower right corner that
visualizes the way the page will appear when
it is finally printed. See also On-screen
formatting.

Previous screen
A jump feature of a WP that produces text that
has passed offscreen from a document in memory. Usually a one- or two-key function, the
previous screen feature helps the user gain
quick access to previously typed text without
having to scroll back to past text.

Primary document
In merging files, the main text to which secondary documents can be added. With the mail
merge function, the body of the letter is
considered the primary document. Names and
addresses are the secondary documents added to
the body of text. Primary documents usually
remain unaltered as a file on disk.

Print buffer
An area that stores data or information. For
instance, some printers provide a buffer so
that the device can store data from the computer for printing while the user continues
operating the computer. By providing additional memory, a print buffer acts as a mediator
between the computer and the printer. But
these buffers are generally limited in memory.
Additional printer buffer accessories, available either as stand-alone units or plug-in
boards, can be purchased separately. They can
provide additional memory ranging from 16K to
256K bytes. These accessories also offer other
advanced features such as data compression,

multiple copies, prestored character strings, status indicators, pause capability, etc. <u>See also</u> Text buffer.

Print density
The number of characters per inch. Although some WPs permit from four to 24 characters per inch, or cpi, to be printed, the numbers depend upon the ability of the individual printer. For instance, many dot-matrix printers can produce a print density of 10, 12, or 17 cpi, while daisy wheel models usually provide 10, 12, or 15 cpi, depending on the print wheel installed at the time.

Print enhancement
A special feature supported by a WP program in conjunction with a printer that changes the final printout visually and physically. Many WPs directly support three basic print enhancements: underlining, boldface, and super- and subscripts. Text marked for enhancement is often displayed on screen in reverse video. Other print enhancements may be performed by embedded commands, provided the printer supports them. <u>See</u> <u>also</u> Enhanced print.

Print format
The parameters assigned to a text file so that it can be printed to a predetermined form. Virtually all WPs provide a special print menu that permits the user to select from default or customized values. Some programs create new documents in the same format as a previous one by just referring to the same suffix. For example, if the file name of a previous document ends in .RPT, a new document with this suffix will adopt that print format. This saves time in setting up a new document and in standardizing all reports, letters, etc.

Print formatting command
An instruction given to the printer. These
instructions usually involve margin settings,
page lengths, page numbers, headers and footers, line spacing, etc. Print formatting commands can be entered in two ways. They can be
selected from a print menu that lists a series
of options or they can be embedded into the
text. See also Dot command, Embedded command,
Print menu.

Print function menu
A list of commands which helps users print
their pages the way they want them. The print
function produces a paper or hard copy of the
document in memory. These functions usually
include such items as single- or double-space,
pause after each page, print an entire document, print specific pages, etc.

Figure P.5 Example of a Print Function Menu

Line spacing (Single, Double)   __

Pause at end of page? (Yes, No)   __

Print from pages   __ to __

Start print at page number   __

Lines per inch (6, 8)   __

Number of copies   __

Print menu
A list of options for controlling the way the
printed page will look. Print menus provide
the user with selections for defining page
length, setting margins, varying justification, controlling headers, footers, pagina-

tion, etc. A print menu has more general listings than the more detailed print function
menu. However, many WPs combine both these
sets of functions and options into one menu.

Print mode
A subprogram of a WP that permits the program
to control the printer to perform certain
tasks. These may include printing selected
records from disks, printing a document from
the screen, formatting a document for printing, printing copies of data disk catalogs,
etc. See also Print menu, Print to disk, Print
to screen.

Print preview. See Previewing.

Print screen
A function key on IBM and similar keyboards
that prints any text on screen onto a page
when pressed in conjunction with the shift
key. In its regular mode, the print screen key
(Prt Sc) produces an asterisk on screen.

Print spooler
A utility program accompanying some WPs that
permits the computer to control operations of
a printer while simultaneously accepting new
data. WPs with print spoolers (Simultaneous
Peripheral Operation On-Line) permit the user
to work with or edit a document in memory
while another is being printed. See also Background mode, Foreground mode.

Print text
An option on some WP menus that causes the
printer to print text either in memory or
stored on disks.

Print to disk
A feature that stores a document on disk in
the same format as it would be printed on
paper. Many WPs convert the file to an ASCII

text file, a standardized code. This procedure adds flexibility to the document, which can then be used with another WP or sent by modem to another machine.

Print to printer
A method of sending a document by way of a WP to a printer that will produce a hard copy (printout). Sometimes this is more easily written about than accomplished. Proper connections must be made between the computer and the printer. Printers usually come with either a parallel or series port, depending on which is required by the computer. Also, the printer must be appropriately "installed" in the WP program. This requires entering a set of printer codes into a utility program of the WP.

Print to screen
A feature of some WPs that depicts on screen how certain configurations of a document, such as page breaks and spacing, will appear on paper. This preview function, however, will not display how certain features such as bold-face, underlining, and other special printer control characters will appear on paper. Usually printer controls such as Pause and Stop also work with the print-to-screen feature. See also On-screen formatting, Previewing.

Print wheel
The changeable type wheel used with a daisy wheel printer. The print wheel allows for font changes as well as for proportional spacing. Various fonts such as italic, Roman, Courier, and Gothic can be inserted easily into the printer so that print style can be changed within a document and on a page. The size of the print can also be changed by using print wheels with either 10- or 12-pitch characters. See also Daisy wheel printer, Pitch.

Printed lines per page
The number of actual text lines, including headers and footers, that are printed out on pages. This should not be confused with paper length, which includes the top and bottom margins. A standard sheet of paper, 8 1/2 x 11 inches, contains 66 lines (six lines per inch), 54 to 58 lines of which are actual text. The printed lines per page default number can usually be modified, as can the page length, depending upon the user's individual needs. These lines may appear on screen, but this does not necessarily mean they will appear on the printout in this format, since line spacing affects the final look. For instance, if the user intends to use double spacing, then the 55 lines appearing on screen before a conventional page break will not be what is printed. Some WPs do display double space on screen, however. See also Page length, Paper length.

Printer
An output adjunct of a computer system that prints text created by the WP or by the computer itself. There are three types of printers: dot-matrix, daisy wheel, and non-impact, the first two being more popular. Non-impact printers include the ink jet, laser, and electrostatic printers. See also Daisy wheel printer, Dot-matrix printer, Electrostatic printer, Impact printer, Ink jet printer, Laser printer, Non-impact printer.

Printer code
A sequence of characters, usually starting with a nonprintable character, designed to tell the printer to perform a special function. Besides printing basic text, some printers can produce special effects such as underlining, fonts of various sizes, boldface, etc. WPs allow the user to enter printer codes to execute these effects. See also Control code,

Printer control character.

Figure P.6   Examples of Printer Codes

```
Alt-+       Underlining On
Alt--       Underlining Off
Alt-S       Shadow Print On
Alt-X       Shadow Print Off
Alt-B       Boldface On
Alt-Z       Boldface Off
Shift-F7    Soft Hyphen
Alt-C       Change Pitch
```

Printer configuration
A procedure provided by many WP programs in
which a particular printer can be set up to
perform special functions incorporated into
the program. For instance, WPs often feature
options such as double and triple space,
changing lines per page, and other such functions. But not all printers perform these
unless they are configured by a utility program built into the WP. There are printers
that provide their own configuration menu as
well as a status report listing standard defaults. See also Installation routine, Printer
installation section, Printer status report.

Figure P.7   A Sample Printer
Configuration Menu

```
Restore Defaults?          ___
Change Form Length?        ___
Change Print Format?       ___
Change LPI?                ___
Change CPI?                ___
Change Char Set?           ___
```

Printer control character
A command sequence or code that, when typed, tells the printer to treat the next character(s) in some special way, e.g., underlining, superscript, etc. Printer control characters are effective only if the codes are installed into the software program, sometimes called the printer installation section. See also Printer code.

Printer disk
A utility program that permits the user to configure and customize the program for any given number of printers. Many WPs incorporate an installation program on one of their disks, while others may devote an entire disk to this purpose. Some WPs can accommodate as few as 25 printer models, while others provide customizing for well over 75. Customizing can range from such basic features as underlining and boldface to esoteric functions such as shadow print, proportional spacing, etc. See also Printer configuration, Printer installation section.

Printer installation section
A utility program on many WPs for entering printer data so that a printer can operate compatibly with the program. Then, when printer control characters are typed, any text following will be treated specially during printout. For instance, boldface, underlining, and other features require the use of controls that must first be installed and accepted into the printer installation section of a WP. See also Installation routine.

Printer interruption
Stopping the printer while it is in operation with the option of continuing or abandoning the printing. WPs offer a variety of terms for these operations, including Stop Printing, Pause Printing, etc. The two major reasons for

halting the printer are for text entry and for changing a ribbon or print wheel. Printer interruption can be accomplished by pressing the escape key, the space bar, or a special series of control keys, depending upon the individual WP.

Printer option
A designation for printing. Different WPs offer a variety of printer options, including vertical spacing (single or double space), justification, underlining, etc. These various options depend on the capabilities of the printer as well as on the features of the WP. See also Print function menu, Print menu.

Printer parameter. See Default parameter, Parameter.

Printer status report
A list of defaults and options provided by certain printers in their manuals to help the user configure the machine for specific tasks.

Figure P.8   Sample Printer Status Report

Form Length	11 inches
LPI	6
CPI	Corr. Quality
LF at Full Line	Yes
Character Set	USA
Interface Type	Parallel

Printer support

The ability of the WP to communicate with the printer. To provide this function, many WPs include a utility program that permits the installation of individual printers. This not only permits the machine to operate in conjunction with the software but allows certain features such as underlining, subscripts, and superscripts to be printed. Some WP programs support a few printers, while others support more than 200. DisplayWrite 2, for example, supports only four printers. On the other hand, WordStar 2000 can operate with 119, while OfficeWriter supports 275 printers! Many WPs such as DisplayWrite, Perfect Writer, and Spellbinder offer printer utilities to accommodate printers not listed in their installation program. See also Installation routine, Printer installation section.

Program

A group or set of instructions or directions that informs the computer how to perform a particular processing task. Programs can be of the commercial or home-made variety and can be written in various languages including machine language, assembly language, and high-level language. WP, database, spreadsheet, and utility programs account for the major share of commercial business software; games and educational programs are extremely popular for the home computer market.

Program disk

The disk that contains the WP program, as opposed to the data disk. A program disk is similar to a textbook, whereas a data disk resembles a workbook. Information is read from the program disk, but written only on the data disk. It is a good idea to protect all program disks, sometimes called master disks, by placing an adhesive tab over the notch on the disk so that no parts get erased or the disk is not formatted by mistake. <u>See</u> <u>also</u> Data disk.

Programmable function key
The ability to replace a program's command characters with others. WPs such as The Final Word that feature programmable function keys allow the user to combine any character, cursor, or control keys to operate different functions. This feature is especially useful when certain unwieldy commands that require pressing multiple keys can be condensed into striking a single function key.

Prompt
A request or message that appears on the display screen and asks for a response. Prompts can refer to editing, printing text, formatting, etc.

Figure P.9   Examples of Prompts

```
                        (a)

    You selected to return to Main Menu
    without saving current changes in
    document.

        PROMPT:          ARE YOU SURE?
         PRESS Y OR N AND PRESS RETURN

                        (b)

    PRESENT FILE ABOUT TO BE OVERWRITTEN!!!

        PROMPT:      Press Return to Continue,
                     Esc to Abandon
```

Proportional spacing
Adjusting the difference between the widths of characters so that the appearance of the hard copy is enhanced or resembles typesetting. Proportional spacing eliminates much of the white or blank space between letters and words on each line. Some reviewers of WPs make a distinction between proportional spacing and true proportional spacing. They reserve the latter for those programs and printers that can allot a different space for characters that have different widths, such as "i" and "m." Not all programs or printers can handle this procedure. Proportional spacing differs from microjustification in that the latter incorporates proportional spacing and full justification. See also Microjustification, Microspace.

Proprietary operating system
A method for storing files. Documents stored in a proprietary operating system cannot be read by other WPs or programs. Text files created by Apple computers use DOS 3.3 files, binary files, Pascal, etc. PFS: Write, although written for the Apple computer, produces text files that are not compatible with Applewriter II or other WPs. A similar incompatibility exists among WPs designed for IBM and compatible machines.

Protect a file. See Lock.

Protocol
Instructions that control the way data bits are sent between a computer and peripherals such as a printer or a disk drive.

PS. See Proportional spacing.

Pull-down menu
A list of options and/or commands available through either function keys or the use of a

"mouse." Pull-down menus, as incorporated into the Macintosh computer and its related software, are available instantly and concealed when not in use. Their commands are frequently simple to understand, since they are written in English; other WPs may use complicated function keys. Also called pop-up menu.

Q

Quarter-line spacing
A vertical spacing feature between single and
half-line spacing offered by very few programs. MultiMate is one program that offers
this function. Not all printers support quar-
ter-spaced lines, and those that do often
produce unpredictable results. See also Line
spacing.

Queuing
A procedure offered by some WPs that "lines
up" files that are to be printed in a given
order. The program, in conjunction with the
computer, seeks the next predetermined file to
be printed as soon as the previous one is
completed. The term "queuing" is often used
interchangeably with chaining or linking.
However, files that are chained or linked are
physically connected; i.e., they are merged
into one long file so that the printer handles
them as such. Queuing, on the other hand,
allows each file to exist as an independent
entity; the WP program refers to each by name,
beckoning each to be printed in the order
determined by the user. WP programs that feature queuing, such as MultiMate, often have
help screens displaying the order in which the
documents will be printed. MultiMate also

offers the user the option of "holding" a file, so that another goes to the "spooler," a storage area which contains the documents before they are printed. See also File chaining, Print spooler.

Figure Q.1 Files Ready for Queuing

Chapter 1   Chapter 2   Chapter 3

File Status:

1. Printing

2. Hold

3. Errors will Blink

Quick menu
A special feature on some WPs designed to help the user make larger than usual moves throughout the document on screen. These commands often include moving the cursor to the top or bottom of the screen as well as moving it to the beginning or end of the document. WordStar, for example, provides a quick menu, as a sub-menu of its main menu, and includes control commands under such topics as cursor movement, delete, miscellaneous, and other menus.

Quit
A function employed by many WPs to take the user from a submenu to the main menu or to leave the program entirely. Manufacturers of WP software usually recommend using the quit command to exit from a program. This helps prevent any possibility of "crashing." Also, it provides a quick and simple way to re-enter the DOS system in many cases. The IBM and

similar systems often use the term "exit."

Quitting without saving
Leaving a working document on screen without storing it on disk. Sometimes the user does not wish to save a particular document, especially if it means writing over the original. Instead of simply shutting down the computer system, the user may, with many WPs, quit or exit without saving.

Figure Q.2   Command Menu

1. Save file, return to Main Menu

2. Save file, resume editing

3. Return to Main Menu, no save

4. Return to editing

5. Print current file

Qwerty keyboard
The conventional layout of keyboard characters found today on virtually all typewriters and keyboard components of computer systems. The Qwerty keyboard, named for the first six keys in the top row of letters, was originally designed to slow down the first typists who plied their trade too well. Their increased skills on the early typewriters rapidly outpaced the capabilities of the machines themselves, causing the keys to jam. With more proficient electronic systems and computer technology, an optional keyboard pattern, the Dvorak layout, was introduced. This new design, which places the most often used characters in more strategic positions, allegedly permits the user to type more quickly. Some

WPs such as The Final Word and other utility programs such as SmartKey II provide the user with the option of reconfiguring the keyboard. There are even some computer systems which offer the owner the option of selecting either of these two keyboards. See also Dvorak keyboard, Keyboard configuration.

R

Ragged margin
A margin which is not justified. Most business letters look more attractive when only the left margin is even or justified; the right margin is then considered ragged or uneven. However, there may be situations in which the left margin requires a ragged look. This is accomplished by justifying only the right margin. Many WPs provide a choice of left, right, center, or full justification. See also Center justification, Full justification, Left justification, Right justification.

Figure R.1   Example of Ragged Left
and Right Margins

```
                    Sometimes
      uneven left and right margins
                    are more
                 eye-catching
            than text that is
            fully justified.
```

RAM
Random Access Memory. This type of memory
allows information to be written in, i.e.,
changed, or read out. Two types of programs
may reside in RAM, resident and transient.
Resident refers to those programs that are
automatically placed in RAM when a disk drive
is activated. Transient programs are disk-
based and loaded into RAM only if the user
chooses to do so. As a storage device, RAM has
two disadvantages. It is temporary and volatile, unlike its counterpart, ROM (Read Only
Memory). Once the machine is shut down, all
data stored in RAM are lost. Also, any information in RAM is subject to the whims of power
outages, electrical storms, power surges, etc.
Therefore, data should be transferred at regular intervals to more permanent memory storage
systems such as disks or tape. ROM, on the
other hand, is permanently installed into the
computer and cannot be altered. See also Resident program, ROM, Transient program.

RAM disk
Software which simulates a disk drive in a
computer's Random Access Memory. Other programs accept the RAM disk as another drive.
Because it works electronically instead of
mechanically as in the case of a floppy disk
drive, the RAM disk operates at a much higher
speed, often as much as 50 times faster. This
time-saving advantage makes it desirable for
running certain programs such as WPs which
periodically have to access other parts of the
program. Once the power is shut off, however,
any data in the RAM disk are lost, whereas
information stored on a floppy disk is pre-
served. Therefore, if the data are to be
saved, they must eventually be transferred to
a conventional disk. Since some disk drives
hold more bytes than some computers, particularly 8-bit systems, RAM disks usually require
the use of 16-bit processors.

Random access memory. See RAM.

Read/write
The ability to read data from and write data into memory. The memory may be disk, tape, or RAM.

Record
A collection of organized data or information in a database. A record, which resembles an index card, includes items of data, where each item is known as a field, such as one line of information on an index card. A file contains a collection of records, similar to a card file made up of a collection of index cards. The information which is placed into a field is called an entry. Many WPs contain a built-in database called mail merge, mail system, etc. See also Entry, File.

Reformat
To set a new left and right margin automatically. See also Paragraph reformatting.

Reforming a paragraph. See Paragraph reformatting.

Remove
A function of some WPs such as PFS: Write to permanently delete a document or file from a disk. Once a document is removed, it cannot be recovered. PFS: Write warns the user that a document is about to be removed. The remove function differs from Clear, which erases the text only in memory and on screen. See also Delete.

Rename
To change the name of a file, usually stored on a disk. Virtually all WPs provide a method for renaming a file. The user should be certain that the new name does not already exist

in the directory of files; otherwise that file
may be overwritten. There are some valid reasons for renaming a file. Its name may be very
similar to another document, which may cause
unnecessary problems; its name may not clearly
identify the contents of the file; or new text
has been added, rendering the original name
meaningless. Some WPs contain a warning during
the process of renaming a file, saying that
the file already exists or that the file will
be overwritten.

Renumber
A function of many programs designed to change
the page numbers of a document on screen.
Renumbering is usually done automatically
whenever a page of text is deleted or added.
Virtually all WPs include a feature that permits a page to go unnumbered, as in the case
of title pages or one-page letters. This procedure is usually accomplished through the use
of dot commands. See also Page numbering.

Repagination
A function that changes the number of lines
per page of a document. See also Renumber.

Repeat key. See Typematic.

Replace
Part of the search and replace function of a
WP in which characters, when found, can be
supplanted by others. The replace function
allows the user to change a current string of
characters to a different one after the program automatically locates each occurrence.
Global Replace automatically changes each
occurrence of the present string throughout a
document with its replacement. Some WPs distinguish between upper-case and lower-case
characters during the search mode. See also
Global search and replace, Search and replace.

Replace mode. <u>See</u> Insert.

Resident program
An operating system routine or program which
is loaded automatically into the computer's
RAM each time the disk drive is activated.
Resident programs usually are assigned specific "housekeeping" chores. Some typical
resident programs include those which allow
the user to run a program, delete a file,
initialize a disk, etc. These programs or
subprograms interpret the input/output routines between the user and the operating system. Some routines are not resident programs.
These are called transient programs. <u>See</u> <u>also</u>
RAM, Transient program.

Response time
The measured time between a request and the
return of data or information from a computer.

Retrieve a document
A function of virtually all WPs which places a
copy of a file on disk and places it into the
memory of a computer for editing, printing,
etc. Regardless of the amount of editing done
to the document, the original remains on the
disk intact. The text in memory is temporary
and can be lost if the computer is turned off.
The altered version can be saved by overwriting the original or by giving it a different
file name, thereby saving both versions.

Return key
The key used to start a new line or paragraph
or to enter blank lines. If the cursor is
placed at the beginning of a line before any
text and Return (or Enter, on some machines)
is pressed, the entire text is usually moved
down one line. If the return key is pressed at
the end of a text line, the cursor moves to
the left margin of the next line for the start
of a new paragraph. With some WPs, Return is

194

also employed to exit the user from the present screen or menu.

Reverse video. See Inverse video.

Reverse word wrap
An editing function in which text moves back or up to a line to fill in blank spaces resulting from characters' having been deleted. Reverse word wrap occurs while the program is in the insert mode. If the WP is operating with the insert mode in the off position, the text on the next line will remain where it is and blank spaces will replace any text that is deleted. See also Insert mode, Word wrap.

Figure R.2   Example of Reverse Word Wrap

(original text)

    The Julian calendar, the basis of the civil calendar now used throughout the world, was derived from the Roman republican calendar as reformed by Julius Caesar.

(with insert mode off)

    The Julian calendar

        was derived from the Roman republican calendar as reformed by Julius Caesar.

(with insert mode on)

    The Julian calendar was derived from the Roman republican calendar as reformed by Julius Caesar.

Revise a file
To overwrite a current file with a more recent
version. The original can be saved by giving
the new file a different file name. Some WPs
such as Easywriter use the revise function to
save an edited file which then replaces the
original one. See also Rename.

RGB color monitor
A video display that provides a separate video
signal for each of the red, green, and blue
picture tube guns. WPs and spreadsheet programs, which usually produce 80 or more columns, require more screen detail than other
software. RGB monitors provide better resolution, or image sharpness, than the standard,
less costly, video, or composite, color monitors which are adequate for color graphics or
40-column displays. See also Color monitor.

Right justification
The alignment of text flush with the right
margin. Not all WPs are capable of producing
right justification. Those that are require
entering this function through the keyboard
and/or a specific menu. Although it is sometimes referred to as full justification, right
and full justification differ: The former
implies ragged left and flush right margins,
while the latter refers to text that is flush
against both margins. Right justification is
important in headers and footers, especially
when the user may prefer to have page numbers,
titles, and chapter headers appear on the
upper or lower right of the printed page,
rather than in the more customary center. See
also Full justification.

Figure R.3   Example of Right Justification

```
                                      Is
                                    your
                                 company
                          moving in the
                       right direction?
```

ROM
Read Only Memory. Information permanently
built into a computer. ROM, which contains
certain operating instructions, cannot be
altered. The user cannot write to ROM. ROM
memory is nonvolatile; unlike its counterpart,
RAM, or Random Access Memory, it cannot be
lost when the machine is shut down or during
power outages. Some computer systems install
WP programs as well as other software into
ROM. See also Memory, RAM.

Routine
A program which handles such tasks as operating the input/output functions, reading the
computer keyboard, reading and writing text to
the printer or display screen, etc. Routines
may emanate from either RAM or ROM.

Ruler line
A horizontal line or bar across the screen,
often simulating a typing bar. The ruler line
usually furnishes left and right margins, tab
markings, spacings in multiples of five or 10,
and a moving figure which signifies the column
number that the cursor is on. It is a useful
feature, especially for those who began their
word processing on a conventional typewriter.
Ruler lines can be turned off on some WPs if
they become distracting. See also Multiple
rulers.

Running title/footer
A title and/or a footer that appears on each page of a document when it is printed out on paper. Many WPs allow for footers and headers as well as page numbers to appear in the center or to the right or left of a page top or bottom. Some WPs permit only a single line, while others can produce multiple-line headers and footers. <u>See</u> <u>also</u> Header, Footer.

S

Save
A command that permits the user to save on disk any data or information that is currently in memory. A document is saved when it is transferred from RAM, a temporary storage area, to a permanent storage medium such as a disk or tape. Many professionals recommend saving files continually to avoid loss of information. They suggest saving data every 20 or 30 minutes. They also recommend that for-matted or initialized disks be prepared in advance, since some WPs do not provide for this within the program. Other WPs save data automatically at regular intervals; still others do not allow the printing of a document until it is first saved on disk. Some WPs require that multiple drive systems state the drive number or letter that will store the document, e.g., [S]ave: Filename,d2. See also Automatic save.

Save-and-print
An option on some WPs that allows the user to select certain printer options and produce a hard copy directly. Some WPs require that a document be saved before printing can occur; then the program returns to its opening or main menu, from which the user can choose the

print option and, if necessary, various print formattings such as number of copies, range of pages, etc. The save-and-print feature avoids these steps by providing direct access to these format files, thereby facilitating the printing of a document.

Save buffer. See Text buffer.

Screen
That part of a computer system that displays part of the information currently stored in the computer's memory. Typical computer screens range in size from nine to 14 inches, with the 12-inch screen the most popular. Screens can come in monochrome or color; the former, because of their higher resolution, are more popular for word processing. A blinking rectangle or horizontal line the size of one character, called a cursor, functions as a pointer and can be moved to any part of the screen. The screen acts like a window that displays portions of information. Some WP programs produce split or multiple screens, permitting the user to view and edit more than one document or different sections of the same document. See also Split screen.

Screen display
What appears on the viewing screen of the monitor connected to the computer. The screen display does not always show exactly what will be printed on paper. Some WPs do format the text on screen; others come reasonably close except that they also display embedded commands that do not print out on paper. The screen display is also known as a video screen, video display, CRT (cathode ray tube), display monitor, etc. Actually few screen displays are reserved only for text; many WPs offer a status line, a menu of options, and a command line. Sometimes all these items tend to clutter up the screen display, occupying

more than a third of the lines. <u>See also</u>
Display screen, Status display, <u>Ruler</u> line.

Figure S.1   Sample Screen Display

```
┌─────────────────────────────────────────┐
│              MAIN MENU                    │
│                                           │
│  1. CURSOR MOVEMENT     4. FORMAT LINES   │
│                                           │
│  2. EDITING FUNCTIONS   5. PRINT FUNCTIONS│
│                                           │
│  3. DISPLAY DIRECTORY   6. ADDITIONAL HELP│
│  ───────────────────────────────────────  │
│                                           │
│  File:Test   Page 1 Line 23 Col 65 Ins: On│
│  ───────────────────────────────────────  │
│                                           │
│  |||5|T||||10||||15||||20||||30|||40|||50 │
│                                           │
│                                           │
│                                           │
│                 (Text)                    │
│                                           │
│                                           │
│                                           │
│                                           │
│  F1 Tabs   F2 L Mrgn   F3 R Mrgn   F4 Indent│
└─────────────────────────────────────────┘
```

Screen formatting. <u>See</u> On-screen formatting.

Screen-oriented print formatting. <u>See</u>
        On-screen formatting.

Screen status line. <u>See</u> Status display.

Scroll
To move text displayed on screen up and down,

thereby showing what precedes or follows the information that currently appears. In some cases the user can also scroll horizontally, displaying text larger than 80 columns per line. Vertical scrolling is important in editing with a WP, whereas horizontal scrolling is necessary when using spreadsheets. In WP programs scrolling can be achieved in different ways, sometimes with the page up and down keys, with the up and down arrow keys, etc.

Search
A feature of many WPs that allows the user to find a character, word, or group of words. Search is usually part of the search and replace feature. See also Search and count, Search and replace, Search options.

Search and count
An option of the search and replace feature found on many WPs. It is designed to count the number of times a word appears in a document. WPs such as Write provide search and count as part of its search and replace function.

Search and replace
A feature that allows the user to look for a character, a word, or a group of words in a document. Once located, the subject of the search can be replaced with another character or word. The search and replace feature can operate forward and backward, through an entire file or part of one, and can replace one or all occurrences. Other options of the search and replace feature include the display of the search string before the command is executed, ignore or match case, and match whole words only. The search and replace function is useful in customizing letters, locating words in a long document, etc. For instance, the name or title of a book can be abbreviated or displayed by a symbol in the writing process. When finished, the user can

then search for each of these occurrences and automatically replace the symbol or abbreviation with the full name or title. See also Global search and replace.

Figure S.2   Typical Search and Replace
with Options

```
   FIND?   Clemons

   REPLACE WITH?   Clemmons

              OPTIONS

  S = Search      B = Search Backwards

W = Whole Words Only    U = Ignore Case

      R = Replace w/o Asking

    E = Replace in Entire File
```

Search options
Choices of finding a word, part of a word, or phrase in a document. Various WPs provide different options or methods of locating items. For example, the user may choose search, automatic search and replace, manual search and replace, count the number of occurrences (of a word or phrase), etc.

Secondary document
A text or file that is merged to a primary or permanent document. A form letter that is a primary document can be formatted so that it is sent to various names and addresses by merging secondary documents with this information into the text body. The number of secondary documents is unlimited. See also Primary document.

Sector
A unit of storage space on a disk. With the
Apple system, each sector contains 256 characters. The catalog, or list of contents on a
disk, displays a file name and its sector
size. See also Catalog, Disk capacity, Disk
space.

Figure S.3   Example of Sector Listings
in Catalog

T 009	LETTER1
T 014	LETTER2
T 157	PROGRAMA
T 072	PROGRAMB
B 084	COPY
A 079	FILE

Security. See Password security, System
security.

Self-booting
A disk that contains DOS as well as a program
such as a WP. If a program or data disk does
not contain DOS it cannot be loaded into the
computer memory until the DOS program is
booted. Some program disks display the message
"bootable" or "self-booting," signifying that
they contain DOS. These programs are also
known as boot/system disks, since they contain
both DOS and the WP.

Self-loading. See Self-booting.

Semi-automatic hyphenation. <u>See</u> Hyphenation.

Sequential access
A procedure of scanning information in which files are accessed in a particular order.

Shadow print
A mode of printing that produces a darker character on the printed page. Each character designated for shadow print is printed twice, the second time slightly to the right. Not all WPs offer this print mode and not all printers are capable of producing it. Shadow print usually requires control symbols that appear on screen but do not print out on paper. The feature differs from boldface, which is created by striking the same character twice in the same position. <u>See</u> <u>also</u> Boldface.

Figure S.4   Example of Shadow Print

> **Shadow print** is created by printing the character a second time off center. This differs from boldface in which each character is struck twice in exactly the same position.

Shared system
A group of terminals connected to one central computer and other equipment on which more than one person can work.

Shift key
A key that operates like a conventional typewriter shift key. When held down, the shift key causes letter keys to be printed in upper case. On computer keyboards, the shift key serves other purposes; WP programs often use it in conjunction with other keys to perform

special functions.

Figure S.5 Example of Shift Key
for Special Functions

Control-J	Cursor left one word
Control-K	Cursor right one word
Shift-F2	Cursor to beginning of line
Shift-F3	Cursor to end of line

Single-stroke mode. See Draft mode.

Slow/speed print
A feature of some WPs such as EasyWriter that permits the printer to be stopped or slowed down. Slow/speed print can also be helpful when printing a text file to the screen, making the document easier to read. This feature, when operated with a serial system, modifies the baud rate.

Smart terminal
A computer system that can do more than send and display data. A smart terminal can usually edit and store documents, communicate with other terminals, and produce graphics.

Soft copy
A duplicate copy of a file on disk that can be transmitted by a modem to a receiver who can then print it out as hard copy. A soft copy of a file has exactly the same contents as a hard copy.

Soft hyphen
A hyphen that is displayed only when a word is to be split at the end of a line. Some WPs

such as WordStar provide soft hyphens, an optional feature that the user may select or reject. When the word is moved to another position after the line is edited, the hyphen is removed automatically. Its counterpart, the hard hyphen, remains no matter where the word occurs. See also Hard hyphen, Hyphenation.

Software
A computer program used in a special application such as word processing, filing, etc. Software directs the computer in a particular order to accomplish special tasks. Software may appear on tapes or disks.

Sort
To arrange data in a predetermined order. Many high-priced WPs are capable of sorting data, especially those programs containing functions such as mail merge and indexing. The sort function can be very complex in its handling of numbers (e.g., zip codes) and the alphabet in ascending or descending order.

Space available. See Available memory.

Space bar
The long horizontal bar at the bottom of the keyboard. When the space bar is pressed, a space is printed on screen. With some WPs the bar will remove a character designated by the cursor and a space will be inserted. With most WPs, however, the space bar has a dual function. In insert mode, it prints a space and moves text to the right. With the insert mode in the off position, the space bar erases any text marked by the cursor without moving any characters that follow.

Special character
A character not normally capable of being printed or addressed by the keyboard. Special characters are often printed through the use

of the control key in combination with other keyboard keys. These characters usually are not capable of being formed on screen, only on the printed page.

Special function key
A key that is neither a character key nor one of the function keys number F1 to F10 (or more on some machines). The special function keys include Escape, Tab, Control, Shift, Alternate, Backspace, Enter or Return, Print Screen, Caps Lock, Numbers Lock, Home, the four arrow keys, End, Insert, Delete, Page Up, and Page Down. These keys perform similar, but not the same, function with various WP programs. Often these keys are combined to augment the number of functions of a program. For instance, pressing Control plus another key will perform one task, while Alternate and the same key may perform a completely different operation. See also Assignable function key, Function key.

Spelling checker
A software program or part of a WP package that compares words of a document to a built-in dictionary list, designating those with any discrepancies. The user then has the option of replacing the words, ignoring the suggestions, or adding the words to the dictionary. As useful as spelling checkers are, they cannot differentiate between homonyms incorrectly used. For example, the program cannot tell the difference between "their" and "there." If these words are misused, the checker will pass these by as long as they are spelled correctly. Spelling checkers that are loaded separately provide prompts for loading text files. More sophisticated spelling checkers can be loaded into the computer along with the WP for complete interaction.

Spelling verify function
A feature of some WPs such as Quick-Text that
permits the user to check the spelling of
words as they are entered into a document on
screen. Some WPs contain a built-in spelling
checker or one that allows a checker to operate with text files that have been created by
that program. Word Proof, although not a full-
fledged WP, provides a built-in dictionary.
The user simply places the cursor on the ques-
tionable word and presses a function key. The
program then displays the word properly
spelled or a list of possible intended words.
Some WPs are written in languages that allow a
spelling checker from another company to scan
their text files. See also Spelling checker.

Split screen
The appearance of more than one document on
the same screen. This feature is especially
useful in reviewing large documents. Some WPs
offer split screen editing, including the
ability to move blocks of text from one file
to the other, to edit each document independently of the other, etc. Split screens are
usually divided horizontally.

Split-screen editing
A feature that allows two portions of a document to be displayed and manipulated simultaneously. With split-screen editing the user
can copy or move text from one place to another; this feature also permits the user to
examine what has been written without having
to leave the present editing position. See
also Multiple-file editing.

Spooled print. See Print spooler.

Standard pitch. See Pitch.

Start control code
An embedded command placed before text intended for a special printing effect. Control
codes appear on screen but not on the printed
page. Start control codes are used for underlining, boldface, sub- and superscript, etc. A
stop control code normally follows the object
text so that the WP returns to its default
mode. See also Control code, Stop control
code.

Figure S.6   Examples of Start and Stop
Control Codes

Both ^Uunderlining^U and ^Bboldface^B
usually require start and stop control
codes.

Startup disk
A software disk with a special program that is
placed into the computer memory before a WP
program is loaded. The startup disk is usually
run as soon as the power is turned on or when
resetting the computer.

Status display
A line provided by many WPs that depicts various kinds of information. Usually the status
display provides the document name; amount of
available space; the current line, column, and
page number, etc. Sometimes the status line
can be removed to give the user more screen
space for text entry or an uncluttered work
area. The line can appear at the top or bottom
of the screen.

Figure S.7   A Typical Status Display

```
File:Test   Line:23   Col:17 Page:3 Ins:On
```

Sticky space. <u>See</u> Hard space.

Stop control code
An embedded command inserted at the end of
text intended for a special printing effect.
Control codes are entered to produce underlining, boldface, and other special effects. The
stop control code ends the effect and returns
the WP to the default commands. Control codes
are visible on screen but do not appear on the
printed page. <u>See also</u> Control code, Start
control code.

Stop justification
The ability of a WP to halt right justification. This is not a particularly serious problem, since most WPs do not use a default
setting for right justification. In other
words, most programs provide a ragged right
column unless right or full justification is
expressly programmed. One exception is Word-
Star 3.3, which has right-justified default.
However, this can be disengaged through one of
the menus before text is entered.

Stop pagination
A command provided by a WP that halts the
automatic numbering of pages during the printing process. This may be important in a document, especially during the printing of the
cover page, which requires no page number, or
the table of contents, which normally takes a
Roman numeral. Pagination is usually halted on
an individual basis by the use of embedded
commands.

Stop printing. <u>See</u> Printer interruption.

Storage disk. <u>See</u> Data disk.

Storage space
The amount of space on a disk that can be used
for saving files and/or programs. Each system
has its own capacity and method of reporting
available space. The amount is governed also
by the method that the disk operating system
employs to write information on the disk and
whether both sides are utilized. Apple, for
example, uses single-sided disks that hold
about 160,000 bytes and measures their units
in sectors. The IBM system and similar machines use both sides of the disk and can hold
more than 360,000 bytes.

Strike over. <u>See</u> Overstrike.

Strike-through
A WP feature that places a line of slashes or
hyphens through printed text. Sometimes, as in
legal documents, it may be important to present a document with strike-throughs to show
changes in the original text. Strike-through
differs from strike-over or overstrike, a
function that replaces existing text with new
characters.

Figure S.8   An Example of Strike-Through

This is a ~~sample~~ ~~that~~ ~~demonstrates~~
~~the~~ ~~use~~ ~~of~~ an example of
strike-through.

String. <u>See</u> Character string.

Style checker
An accessory program that searches for such
items as passive verbs, clichés, wordiness,
awkward phrasing, stylistic problems, etc.
Some style checkers offer alternative words or
phrases which may then be substituted for the
original word or phrase. See also Grammar
checker, Spelling checker, Thesaurus.

Style sheet
A customized form that a user can apply to
future documents so that a standard can be
achieved. A style sheet is created separately,
independent of a document, and usually includes such formatting information as tabs,
line spacing, headers and footers, indentations, justification, etc. A style sheet can
be as simple as a form letter with preset top,
bottom, left, and right margins, or as complex
as a customized inventory form. See also
Boilerplating.

Subdirectory
A file containing the names and locations of
other files on the disk but not the standard
or volume directory. Subdirectories are useful, especially in relation to a hard disk.
They can help organize numerous files by category. Instead of one long listing of 100
files, for instance, the directory may contain
20 files under WP, 15 under LETTERS, another
24 under REPORT, etc. Following this procedure, the user need not search through the
100 files, only the few subdirectories. When
one of these is called to the screen, all the
files in that particular subdirectory are
listed. See also Directory.

Figure S.9 Subdirectories Listed
in Main Directory

```
Volume in drive B has no label
Directory of     B:\

COMMAND    COM    17792    10-20-85    12:01p
ANSI       SYS     1664    10-20-85    12:01p
WORDPROC          <DIR>     4-22-86     8:21p
LETTERS           <DIR>     5-18-86    11:04a
REPORTS           <DIR>     5-22-86     9:48a
```

Figure S.10 Contents of One Subdirectory

```
Volume in drive B has no label
Directory of B:\wordproc

.          <DIR>            4-22-86     8:21p
..         <DIR>            4-22-86     8:21p
CHAP1               9784    4-23-86     9:42a
CHAP2              11093    4-24-86    11:07a
CHAP3              27537    4-26-86     8:13p

    5 file(s)   297513 bytes free
```

Subfunction
A part of a menu or submenu of functions, usually called to screen by moving the down arrow until the desired subfunction is high-lighted or by typing the first letter of the function. Subfunctions are mainly the products of menu-driven WPs. The user selects a func-tion from a list of options provided by the main menu. These may include Print, Edit, Format, etc. If Print is selected, for exam-ple, a submenu of print functions appears on the screen. Such items as single or double space, number of copies, and other options are known as subfunctions.

Submenu
A list of functions or options derived from a menu or system menu. Submenus may contain subtopics relating to print, edit, format functions, etc. For instance, a format submenu may contain such options as page length, top margin, bottom margin, left margin, etc. Options may be changed or selected in various ways, such as typing the number choice, moving down the list with the Arrow keys, pressing Return or Enter, etc.

Figure S.11   Example of a Submenu

```
        BLOCK FUNCTION MENU

B = Begin Block        E = End Block

C = Copy Block         D = Delete Block

M = Move Block         S = Save Block

    Select Letter and Press Return
```

Subscript
A character printed below the base line. Some WPs have the ability to direct the printer's vertical spacing so that it prints equations or symbols off-line, as in the case of H_2O. The number "2," called a subscript, requires a special printer code or embedded command so that it can be printed. Although a particular WP may offer this feature, not all printers are capable of producing subscripts. See also Superscript.

Figure S.12   Subscripts

(as they appear on screen)

Hydrogen sulphide (HAlt-S2Alt-SS) is
different from HAlt-S2Alt-SSOAlt-S4Alt-S.

(as they appear on printed page)

Hydrogen sulphide (H_2S) is different

from H_2SO_4.

Superscript
The ability of a WP to control a printer's
vertical spacing so that it produces one or
more characters above the base line. To print
68° or footnotes, for example, the "o" and
reference figures must be produced off-line.
These characters, called superscripts, require
special codes or embedded commands so that
they can be printed. Many WPs offer this feature, but not all printers can support it. See
also Subscript.

Figure S.13   Superscripts

(as they appear on screen)

^S1^SThe temperature may fluctuate from
72^So^S to 78^So^S.

(as they appear on printed page)

[1]The temperature may fluctuate from

72° to 78°.

Supplemental dictionary
An additional dictionary operating as part of
a spelling checker. Spelling checkers contain
a main dictionary that is the major program
against which a document is checked for spelling errors. Supplemental dictionaries contain
additional words, technical terms, proper
nouns, and other forms of common nouns including plurals, prefixes, and suffixes. These
optional dictionaries can also be created by
the user to include specific terms and names
relating to a particular document, although
this collection of entries is usually called a
custom or personal dictionary and occupies a
separate file on disk. See also Dictionary,
Custom dictionary.

Syntax
Grammatical rules under which a computer language functions. If the syntax of that system
is not followed, a user will not be able to
communicate with the computer or the WP program, because they will not comprehend the
instructions that are entered. Computer systems are very exact in the commands and other
information they will accept. If, for example,
a colon is required after a disk drive letter
is entered and you use a comma, the system
will not comprehend the command.

Syntax error
A DOS screen error message that appears when
an incorrect command sequence is entered. The
syntax of the computer system must be followed
exactly; check the instruction manual. See
also Syntax.

System menu. See Main menu.

System security
A method designed to prevent unauthorized
persons from gaining access to confidential

documents. To maintain maximum security, the program permits the owner to assign a secret password to each document.

T

Tab
A method of formatting a document; also, a means of moving the cursor. Tabs control indentation as well as set up columns. With some WPs they are used for scrolling horizontally, editing, proofreading, etc. Other WP programs assign the tab key to move the cursor from one option to another in submenus.

Figure T.1   Use of the Tab Key in a Submenu

```
Line Spacing (S/D) S   Number of Copies 1

Start Page          1   End Page          1

Printed Lines      55   Page Length      66

Header:

Footer:


        PRESS TAB TO CHANGE OR ADD.
           THEN PRESS RETURN
```

Table of contents function
A feature of some WPs capable of searching for
words or phrases marked in a document by the
user and arranging them automatically in a
table of contents format. The table of contents function usually works in conjunction
with the index function. See also Index.

Telecommunications
The transmission of data by electronic means,
usually over telephone lines. A WP at one
location can communicate with another WP or
computer stationed in another part of the
country or world. Both computers must use a
similar modem. See also Modem.

Template
A predetermined format or overlay such as a
form letter that is designed so that other
data or information from other files can be
inserted easily. Templates are used extensive-
ly with legal, accounting, medical, and insur-
ance software where standard forms are often
required. See also Boilerplating, File-to-file
access, Keyboard template.

Temporary file
A document previously saved on disk solely for
the purpose of loading it into a current document in memory. Some WPs can lift copies of
paragraphs or blocks of text from other files
or from the same document and place them anywhere within the current text. This is more
commonly known as boilerplating. However,
other programs do not have the capability of
full boilerplating. Creating temporary files
accomplishes this function to some extent by
storing these blocks as separate files and
then adding them to the current document. See
also File-to-file access.

Text
A combination of letters, numbers, and punc-

tuation marks formatted into readable characters. In word processing, "text" may refer to
what is on screen or what is printed out.

Text alignment
Moving text to close up blank spaces on lines
and between words. In some WPs, when text is
added, changed, or deleted, line lengths become irregular; the text alignment function,
similar to paragraph reformatting, corrects
this. It is also used following margin changes
and indentations. Some WPs such as WordStar
have a command for this function, while others
align text automatically. With programs utilizing the former approach, a list of commands
appears on screen in addition to a command
line, and the user selects the align text
command. See also Paragraph reformatting.

Text area. See Work area.

Text buffer
A part of the computer memory used to temporarily store characters for eventual block
move, block copy, etc. Ordinarily, each time
new text is stored in the buffer, old text
residing there is replaced and deleted. Text
remains in the buffer during editing, formatting, and menu manipulations. The buffer,
sometimes referred to as a block buffer, re-
tains information as long as the system power
is on. When the power is shut off, text in the
buffer as well as that on screen is permanently lost. See also Print buffer.

Text deletion
The ability of a WP to remove a character,
word, line, sentence, paragraph, or other
block of text. Each WP offers its own range of
deletions as well as its own procedures. Some
are quite limited in removing text; others,
such as WordStar 2000, encompass the entire
spectrum listed above, including the capacity

to undo or restore erased text. Generally, the more costly the program, the more sophisticated its text deletion options. The methods vary from the use of the delete key, the backspace key, or a combination of keys. Text deletion may also depend on the mode of the WP program, such as Insert, etc. See also Delete.

Figure T.2 Sample Commands to Delete
Character, Word, Line, etc.

Back Space Key	Character Left
Control F	Character Right
Control L	Word Left
Control W	Word Right
Control Y	Line
Control S	Sentence
Control P	Paragraph

Text disk. See Data disk.

Text editor
That part of a WP program which controls how text is placed into the memory of the computer and shown on the display screen. All WPs have text editors. The text editor permits inserting and correcting text; deleting characters, words, lines, etc.; and moving text to other parts of the screen or document. The counterpart of the text editor, the text formatter, controls such aspects as margins, tabs, and line spacing. See also Format command, Text formatter.

222

Text field. <u>See</u> Work area.

Text file
A document created by means of a WP and saved
on a permanent medium such as a disk or tape.
Not all text files are compatible with other
WPs. Some have to be converted before they can
be loaded into or edited by other programs.
The problem stems from the various languages
used to create text files. For example, WPs
such as The Write Choice and Bank Street
Writer utilize binary files. These must be
converted, using a built-in utility program,
before they can work with other WPs such as
Screenwriter II. The Write Stuff, another WP,
does not use the standard ASCII format. Because it creates files in its own format
(called Writer Files), its files must be converted by a utility that the program provides
for this purpose. Text files cannot be independently booted or loaded into memory to be
displayed on screen; they are dependent upon
their respective WP program. Although ASCII
files occupy more space on a disk than binary
files do, they have the advantage of being
compatible with most electronic communications
systems. Other file configurations must first
be converted. <u>See</u> <u>also</u> File.

Text file conversion. <u>See</u> Converting text
        files.

Text formatter
That part of a WP that aligns text on screen
or on the printed page according to predetermined parameters. Some of the functions of the
text formatter include the adjustments of the
left, right, top, and bottom margins of text;
the setting of tabs, headers, footers, and
line spacing; and the control of boldface,
underlining, and super- and subscripts. The
counterpart of the text formatter, the text
editor, controls the manipulation of text. <u>See</u>

<u>also</u> Text editor.

Figure T.3 Sample Menu for
Formatting Text

1. Page Length	66
2. Top Margin	6
3. Lines per Page	54
4. Left Margin	10
5. Right Margin	75
6. Double Space	NO
7. Change Options	

SELECT NUMBER: _   PRESS RETURN

Text insertion. <u>See</u> Insert.

Text insertion mode
A method of entering text into a document on
screen. Text insertion consists of two modes,
nondestructive and destructive insert. The
former moves old text to the right of the
cursor as new characters are entered. The
latter is an overwrite mode that replaces old
text with new information. <u>See</u> <u>also</u> Insert.

Text object
Any character, word, sentence line, paragraph,
viewscreen, buffer, etc. Some WPs use commands
to select a particular text object that is
then edited by further commands. <u>See</u> <u>also</u>
Mode-oriented.

Text string. See Character string.

Text window. See Window.

Thermal printer. See Non-impact printer.

Thesaurus
A WP accessory program that produces a list of
synonyms for a given word. A thesaurus usually
works from within the WP. This differs from
many spelling checkers that are set into motion after a document has been completed. As
text is entered, the user may decide to use a
substitute for a particular word. The cursor
is placed somewhere on this entry, and the
thesaurus is brought into play, displaying an
assortment of similar words. After the user
selects one of these options, the word is
transferred to the text automatically. See
also Grammar checker, Spelling checker, Style
checker.

Thimble
A formed-character printer that uses a printing element in the shape of a thimble. Thim-
bles, usually interchangeable, are available
in different fonts and sizes, such as Roman,
Gothic, and italic. There are two types of
printing elements used by formed-character
printers, the thimble and the daisy wheel. See
also Daisy wheel printer, Letter-quality.

Third-party software
Programs created and published by individuals
or companies other than those that distribute
computers. For example, IBM distributes the WP
Displaywriter II, while Apple Computer sells
its AppleWriter II and AppleWorks; third-party
packages designed for these computers include
PFS: Write, WordStar, Perfect Writer, etc. WP
programs released by the computer company may
be more convenient to purchase, but they are
not necessarily better either in ease of

learning or in the number of advanced features
they offer. Sometimes the hardware company
adapts a third-party package and relabels it
as its own.

Tidy and compress
A WP feature that helps to remove blank spaces
resulting from the editing process. Tidy and
compress deletes these blanks and moves text
to the left, even from another line if necessary, to fill the empty spaces. See also Compress, Paragraph reformatting.

Figure T.4   Example of Tidy and Compress

(before editing)

There are many different reasons
for using the tidy and compress function
in typing with a WP.

(after editing)

There are many   reasons
for using   tidy and compress
with a WP.

(after tidy and compress)

There are many reasons for using
tidy and compress with a WP.

Toggle
A switch that can be turned on and off. Toggle
codes are used in many WP programs to control
printer functions such as underlining, boldface, etc. For instance, to toggle the superscript function, the user must first type a
control or escape code to turn on the function
and another set of codes to turn the feature

off. A toggle command is also used in many WPs for markers in moving blocks of text. One toggle command is usually placed at the beginning of the text to be moved and another at the end to cancel the command. Toggle commands can usually be turned on and off using the same keys. Each WP employs a different series of codes. See also Start control code, Stop control code.

Figure T.5   Some Toggle Commands

Shadow Print On	Control-SP
Shadow Print Off	Control-SQ
10 Pitch On	Control-PN
10 Pitch Off	Control-PF

Top margin
The amount of space, measured in inches or line spaces, from the top of a sheet of paper to the first line of print. Top margins can be set by either the printer or the WP program. A WP usually designates a top margin in line spaces.

Top of form
A printer function that advances or feeds paper to the top of the next sheet. This is useful in setting the top of the page for continuous-form paper.

Track
That part of the magnetic medium, such as disk or tape, that is written upon and is accessible to the read/write head of a disk or tape drive.

Tractor feed
A system that moves continuous-form paper through a printer. Sprocket wheels are employed to engage the perforations on the left and right margins of the paper. Some printers come equipped with the tractor-feed mechanism. For other printers, tractor feed assemblies are available as an option at extra cost. See also Paper feed device.

Transfer
An option or submenu on some WPs that permits the user to format a disk, save the text, retrieve a file from a disk, clear text from the screen, rename a file, delete a file from a disk, print a document, or quit the program. Bank Street Writer is one such WP that utilizes Transfer to provide the above options. The term "transfer" can also refer to changing a WP file into a standard DOS file and, conversely, changing DOS files into those that can be edited by that particular WP program.

Transient program
An operating system program that resides on disk and can be loaded into RAM to perform certain routines. Transient programs include those that calculate the amount of remaining space on a disk, copy programs, and assembly programs. These may be supplied by the computer manufacturer or by third-party companies. They are similar to utility programs. A resident program, on the other hand, automatically loads into RAM when the disk drive is turned on. See also Resident program, Utility program.

Transpose command
A feature offered by relatively few WPs that allows the user to reverse the position of two characters. Very often a typist, particularly a fast one, "overtypes" and reverses two letters. The transpose function corrects this.

The user simply places the cursor on the first of the two characters and presses the proper command, thereby reversing the position of the characters.

Figure T.6   Example of a Transpose Command

(before)

The transpose command simplife̲is reversing any to̲w characters.̲

(after)

The transpose command simplifies reversing any two characters.

True proportional spacing
A procedure for spacing characters on a line so that some letters take more space than others. For example, "m" and "w" require more width than the letters "i" and "l." Some users of WPs confuse proportional spacing, a method that adds additional full spaces between words so that a line of text can be fully justified, with true proportional spacing, in which each space is unique to the width of the character. See also Microjustification, Microspace, Proportional spacing.

Type face. See Font.

Type position pointer
A feature found on some WPs that provides a moving symbol across a ruler line to coincide with the typing or cursor position. WPs such as VisiWord and PFS: Write utilize the type position pointer, which allegedly helps to ease the transition from typewriter to WP. Many other WPs simply display a column number

that identifies the horizontal position of the cursor or the character.

Figure T.7   Example of a
Type Position Pointer

```
--------------------------------------------------
  |||| : |||| : |||| : ⊥||| : |||| : |||| : |||| :
--------------------------------------------------
```

In the above example, the cursor rests on column 16 and will move forward as text is entered.

Typematic
A key that repeats its character automatically when it is held down. All keys on the computer keyboard are typematic keys. See also Keyboard.

Typeover. See Insert.

Typewriter mode
A feature of some WPs that permits the user to have direct access to the printer. The computer, in effect, emulates a typewriter. Typewriter mode, sometimes called direct print or hot print, can be a very practical feature, especially when the user wishes to fill out forms, address individual envelopes, etc. Some WPs give the user a choice. Text can be transmitted directly, one keystroke at a time, or text can be edited line by line before it is sent to the printer.

U

Uncase
The ability of a WP to change the case of one
or more characters. A rather rare feature,
Uncase can be helpful when the user wishes to
change a title or subheading from all capitals
to small letters. A second command can then
change the first letter back to upper case.
The Final Word, for example, uses the command
^U to execute Uncase.

Undefine
A command used with some WPs such as XYWrite
to restore a block of text that has been
defined, or marked, for moving, copying, or
deleting.

Undelete
A term used by some WPs to describe the resto-
ration of segments of deleted text. Sometimes
the user may accidentally or deliberately
remove text. Usually this information is lost
forever, but with the undelete function the
text can be resurrected. Some WPs use this
feature to move blocks of text from one place
in the document to another. The block of text
is marked, deleted, and then undeleted at
another location designated by the cursor. The
undelete function often has a stipulation that

231

no Save or Delete has been executed between the original erased text and the time it is to be recalled. See also Block move.

Underlining
The placement of a solid or broken line beneath a printed character or group of characters. Each WP uses its own method to produce underlining either on the screen or on paper. For example, some programs place control characters before and after the text to be underlined; others are capable of displaying the function on screen; while still others show the marked text in reverse video. In many cases underlining, or underscoring as it is sometimes called, must be installed into a utility program of the WP before it can operate properly. Some WPs such as Samna Word III can produce three variations of underlining: a solid line, a broken line, and a double line.

Figure U.1   Underlining
with Control Characters

```
(as it appears on screen)

    ^UUnderlining^U is sometimes pro-
duced by using ^Uspecial control char-
acters^U that appear on screen but not
in the printout. Other WPs have the ca-
pacity to display underlining right
on the screen.

(as it appears on printed page)

    Underlining is sometimes produced
by using special control characters that
appear on screen but not in the print-
out. Other WPs have the capacity to pro-
duce underlining right on the screen.
```

Underscoring. <u>See</u> Underlining.

Undo

A sophisticated WP feature which by the use of a few keystrokes can recall text that has been accidentally deleted. With most WPs, when text is erased or deleted from a document, it cannot be reinstated. Undo, therefore, is a useful tool. Some WPs, such as AppleWriter II, provide a feature which permits removing a limited amount of text and placing it in a buffer. Later, if this text is desired, it can be retrieved and placed anywhere in the document. However, this is not exactly the same as the undo feature.

Figure U.2   Example of the Undo Feature

(original text)

The undo feature is helpful if the user decides to reclaim text that has been removed. This can save retyping. Not all WP programs, however, offer this feature.

(third sentence deleted)

The undo feature is helpful if the user decides to reclaim text that has been removed. This can save retyping.

(after Undo)

The undo feature is helpful if the user decides to reclaim text that has been removed. This can save retyping. Not all WP programs, however, offer this feature.

Unformatted file

A document stored without formatted information such as tabs, margins, etc. Each line of
an unformatted file is like an individual
entity. All or part of the file can be loaded
or merged into other files, etc. Unformatted
files, when loaded into memory, look like
formatted files. Some WPs make clear distinc-
tions between the two, especially in terms of
editing. Formatted files cannot be divided or
inserted into other files while their counter-
parts are more flexible in their loading,
transferring, etc.

Uninstall

To remove an installation process from a commercial software program for the purpose of
copying, etc. Some WPs, for instance, are
copy-protected, allowing only a limited number
of copies to be made. If one of these copies
fails, uninstalling the WP program permits
making an additional copy. This process is
particularly useful and necessary if the user
wishes to copy the program onto a hard disk.
It can later be transferred to a soft disk by
uninstalling it.

Unlabel

To remove particular markers or parameters
from text or a block of text. For instance,
many WPs require that a block of text be
labeled before it can be copied, moved, or
removed. A WP may mark this block by displaying it in inverse video. The markers and the
inverse video can be removed with the unlabel
function. Some programs, such as WordStar,
make this task very simple, requiring only
that the same labeling symbol be struck over
the existing one.

Figure U.3   Using the Unlabel Feature

(labeling a block)

Alt-BControl characters usually
surround portions of text destined to
be moved or removed. These can be removed using the unlabel function.Alt-B

(unlabeling a block by placing
cursor at control characters
and pressing those keys)

Alt-BControl characters usually
surround portions of text destined to
be moved or removed. These can be removed using the unlabel function.Alt-B

(the block of text unlabeled)

Control characters usually
surround portions of text destined to
be moved or removed. These can be removed using the unlabel function.

Unlock
To remove the protection of a file so that it
can be overwritten or deleted. Locked files
cannot be erased. To unlock a file the user
should locate the same menu which was used to
protect the file. An unlocked file differs
from a disk with protection tab on it. The
former can be erased if the disk is erased,
re-initialized, or reformatted, while the
tabbed disk cannot be written over until the
tab is removed. See also Lock.

Unprotect a File. See Lock, Unlock.

235

Unsupported printer utility

A WP utility program designed to configure printers so that certain features will operate smoothly between the machine and the WP. Usually a WP supports a number of popular printer models. All the user has to do is select a model from a list of printers and the program does the rest. In the case of other models, a utility built into the WP program helps to configure those machines.

User-defined file

A document saved on disk which contains such items as configuration parameters, macro definitions, tab stop positions, and other data created as an individual file by the user. User-defined files can usually be loaded automatically whenever the system is turned on or loaded during editing. Many WPs provide user-defined files, which are sometimes known as glossaries or libraries. Data are entered only once into each file, simplifying certain repetitive tasks such as configuring the printer, formatting, etc.

User-defined function key

A key utilized, usually with another, to recall a predetermined series of keystrokes or commands. WPs often assign the control key plus a numeral as user-defined keys to accelerate a complex series of keystrokes. See also Programmable function key.

User friendly

Any software or hardware that is easy to learn and use. WPs that are considered user friendly are those with on-screen help, mnemonic commands, and extensive help menus.

Utility program

A program, often within a WP, that performs a useful or practical task such as customizing the WP to operate with a particular printer,

customizing the screen display for a color
monitor, saving a glossary or macro file, etc.
These types of utility programs are often
called installation programs. Utilities also
perform systems-level functions such as print
spooling, telecommunicating, and recovering
deleted files. Utility programs may be on
separate disks, part of the main WP program,
or an optional program designed to operate
with a specific WP but published by a separate
company.

Figure U.4   Sample Menu of Utility Programs

```
   1. Printer Selection Menu

   2. Printer Configuration

   3. Color/Mono Monitor Configuration

   4. Other Installations


   Select a number and press Enter: _
```

V

Variable character width. <u>See</u> Micro-
    justification.

Variable pitch. <u>See</u> Microjustification.

Variable width. <u>See</u> Microjustification.

Vertical block
Columnar text designed for manipulation by a
WP. A vertical block of text can be sorted in
ascending or descending order by some WPs such
as WordStar 2000. Some programs can add, sub-
tract, multiply, and divide vertical blocks of
figures, depending on the block commands of
the particular WP. <u>See also</u> Block, Block copy,
Block editing, Block move.

Vertical motion index
The amount of vertical space allotted to a
line. By using vertical motion index, the user
can print lines in increments of 1/48 of an
inch. Vertical lines are measured in lines per
inch, or lpi. The default value for most WPs
and printers is 6 lpi, allowing 66 lines per
standard 8 1/2 X 11-inch page (11 X 6 = 66
lines). This lpi value is sometimes known as
page interval, or PI. AppleWriter II uses this
terminology to set the total number of lines

from the top to the bottom of a page. Default values, however, can be changed to suit special printing needs. See also Horizontal motion index.

Vertical scroll
The ability of a WP to move text on screen up or down. Vertical scroll is important in editing, since it allows the user to view the text which precedes and follows any anticipated changes. This function is usually performed either with the arrow keys or with the page up and down keys. The greater the flexibility of the vertical scroll (e.g., to top or bottom of screen, to beginning or end of a document, the more useful the WP program. See also Scroll.

Vertical slide
A technique that permits the user to move text up and down the page. Each time this command is activated, a line is pushed down the page and a blank space is inserted. Also, all subsequent lines are moved down, resulting in an increase in the total number of text lines. The number of lines per page, however, is not affected. Vertical slide also allows a line of text to move up the page. In this instance, it covers the current text, overwriting the line. Although this appears to be a simple method of deleting a line, the original text cannot be retrieved. Each time a line is moved up, one less line of text appears on the page. With some WPs such as Format II, pressing the "V" with the cursor on the line which is to be moved activates the vertical slide command. The "+" key is used to slide a line down the page while the "-" key slides a line up the page.

Figure V.1   Using the Vertical Slide
Function

(before vertical slide)

    The vertical slide is a quick way
to remove blank lines after text has
been deleted.

It has another function.
This function can also add a line to a
page.

(after vertical slide)

    The vertical slide is a quick way
to remove blank lines after text has
been deleted. This function can also add
a line to a page.

Vertical spacing
A printer option activated from within a WP
which control such measurements as the size
and length of each page as well as other
parameters. Vertical spacing includes paper
length, page length, top margin, bottom margin, single/double spacing, etc. Some WPs
provide a wider array of choices such as multiple-line spacing of up to seven.

Video display terminal. See Monitor.

Virtual memory
A method some WPs employ to allow the user to
work on files larger than the memory of the
computer. The program periodically exchanges
information between the data disk and machine
memory. Some WPs are only memory-based, which
limits the working file size to the capacity
of the computer's memory. A virtual memory
program such as Perfect Writer is disk-based,

increasing the document length to the capacity of the disk. See also Disk-based WP, Memory-based WP.

Volatile storage
The storage of data, information, or files in a memory device which is temporary. Volatile storage implies that the data may be subject to loss if the power fails or is turned off accidentally. The Random Access Memory in a computer is considered volatile for these reasons. Nonvolatile storage devices include floppy disks, hard disks, and tape. See also RAM, ROM.

W

What-you-see-is-what-you-get. <u>See</u> WYSIWYG.

White space
The part of a printed document that extends beyond the left and right margins or the space on both sides of a printed character. In the first instance, white space is controlled by the margin settings. In the second, propor-tional spacing or microjustification can limit the amount of white space between characters and words so that the finished document has a more appealing look to it.

Figure W.1   Example of White Space
with Full Justification

> Some WPs offer full justification or proportional spacing by adding extra spaces between words instead of utilizing microjustification to produce true proportional spacing.

Widow
A paragraph which starts on the last line of a page. Since this layout appears awkward on the

printed page, some WPs allow the user to format pages so that these lines are carried over
to the next pages. See also Orphan.

Figure W.2   Example of a Widow

(bottom of page)

Some writers prefer a WP program
that moves widows (the first line of a
paragraph which begins on the bottom of
a page) to the next page.
This makes for a better appearance

Wild card character
A character which can be utilized to represent
any other character. This feature can help
locate names or words of whose spelling the
user may not be certain. To check a document
for all occurrences of the name Reisner or
Riesner, the user would enter: R**sner. The
program would then find all the words and
names with seven characters which start with
"R" and ends with "sner." A wild card character is sometimes called a global character.
See also Any-length character, Search and
replace, Wild card search.

Wild card search
A method of locating portions of words or
phrases within a document. Some WPs use a
special symbol to denote the unknown characters. PFS: Write, for example, utilizes two
periods (..). If "th" is entered in the search
mode followed by two periods (th..) the program will find the next word which begins with
"th." Or, in some wild card searches, if the
first and last letters of a word are entered
with unknown characters inserted such as
"t..m" a list of all possible four-letter

words appears beginning with "t" and ending with "m." See also Global search and replace, Search and replace.

Figure W.3   Example of Wild Card Search

```
          Find: t..m

        (screen displays)

            team

            term

            tram

            them
```

Window
A separate portion of the display screen which shows data or information from another part of the file or from additional files. Some WPs such as Word can display up to eight windows simultaneously. Windows give the user a wide range of applications. The same document can appear in two windows, different parts scrolled separately, and blocks of text moved from one to the other. Besides the cut-and-paste function, windows can be used for storing notes, editing, etc. Also, a WP program can occupy one window while a graph rests in another and a spreadsheet appears in a third. The user can then draw data from the latter two while writing a report in the first. See also Split screen.

Word
A unit of information contained in the memory of a computer. Each word in a microcomputer consists of eight or 16 bits, and in a main-

frame system, of 32 bits.

Word count
The ability of a WP to count the number of
times a selected word appears or to count the
total number of words in a document. Some WPs
can only perform the latter function. The word
count function ordinarily operates from within
the search and replace feature of a WP.

Word processing option
An additional program, either accompanying the
WP package or purchased from third-party software publishers, which is designed to work
with the WP. Some WP options include style
checkers, grammar checkers, spelling checkers,
and thesauruses.

Word processor
Hardware and/or software which permits text to
be electronically manipulated, corrected, and
reproduced. WP hardware consists of a keyboard-operated terminal, a video display, and
a magnetic storage device. A computer specifically designed for word processing is usually called a dedicated word processor. WP software consists of two parts: a text editor and
a text formatter. Through the control of a
cursor, the text editor can insert, delete,
and correct text. The text formatter prepares
the information to desired specifications
before it appears in print.

A WP permits the user to make changes
easily. Words and paragraphs can be added or
deleted. Documents can be proofread and corrected on screen before they are printed on
paper. In addition, the computer allows the
document to be stored and recalled as often as
desired. Form letters can be created and
merged with specific mailing lists. See also
Dedicated WP.

Word wrap
A feature that permits text to be entered without having to utilize the return key at the end of each line. In the insert mode, when text is added to or deleted from a document, the word wrap feature usually adjusts the text by moving it to the right and onto the next line or to the left, filling the gap made by deletions. One problem with word wrap concerns hyphenation. The position of the text is constantly being altered during editing; one result is that hyphenated words maintain their hyphens even when they reappear in the middle of a line. Some WPs offer features that distinguish between "soft" and "hard" hyphens to help cope with this problem. Word wrap has been universally accepted as a time-saving device and has been known to accelerate typing by as much as 15 percent. See also Hard hyphen, Hyphenation, Insert mode, Soft hyphen, Tidy and compress.

Figure W.4   Example of Word Wrap

(before)

Word wrap is a useful function for filling in gaps when unwanted text is removed   This task is usually accomplished automatically.

(after)

Word wrap is a useful function for filling in gaps when unwanted text is removed. This task is usually accomplished automatically.

Work area
A section of the display screen allotted to
the text or document. It is in this space that
editing and formatting occurs. WPs divide
their screens in various ways, but they often
have in common a status display, a command
line, and a work area. Work areas themselves
differ greatly from program to program. Some
like PFS: Write resemble a blank page with
only a ruler line, similar to that of a page
in a typewriter. Others, like WordStar, are
cluttered with a help menu which occupies
approximately the top third of the screen and
a command line across the bottom. Many of
these WPs, however, have a feature which can
remove the help screen if the user finds it
distracting. See also Command line, Display
screen, Ruler line, Status display, Help
menu.

Working copy
A temporary work space in the memory of the
computer holding a document until it is stored
or saved on a disk. A working copy can consist
of a new document or one which has been retrieved from a disk for editing purposes.
Since the condition of the working copy may
sometimes be precarious because of potential
power failures and other possible accidents,
the document should be saved periodically. In
this way only a part of the entire working
copy is lost when disaster strikes. The term
"working copy" can also refer to a duplicate
of the WP program disk. A working copy should
be made of the master program. The user then
stores the original in a safe place and uses
the copy on a daily basis.

Workspace
The amount of memory that is available to
contain the text to be edited or reviewed. The
size of the workspace is usually measured in
kilobytes, such as 64K, 256K, etc. Workspace

is not ordinarily a problem with hard disks
whose capacities are measured in megabytes (10
MB, 20 MB, etc.). Many computers can have
their memory or workspace expanded by the
addition of peripheral cards. For instance, a
machine with 256K can be extended to 640K with
the appropriate accessories. Because of the
recent advances in software and the sophisticated functions available by each, many of
today's commercial programs require a larger
workspace size than those supplied with earlier computers.

Workstation
Any terminal with a display screen and a keyboard.

Wraparound. See Word wrap.

Write
To move information such as text or a document
from the computer memory to an external destination such as a floppy or hard disk drive, a
printer or a modem. "To write to disk" is a
popular expession used in documentations and
computer magazines.

Write-protect
A method of guarding data written on a storage
disk. An 8-inch disk is write-protected by
removing an adhesive tab from its jacket. A 5
1/4-inch floppy is write-protected by putting
a similar tab over the notch in the side of
the disk. Information on disks that have been
write-protected cannot be erased or written
over. Neither can these disks be formatted or
initialized.

WYSIWYG
Short for "what-you-see-is-what-you-get."
Some WPs print text exactly the way it appears
on screen. Other programs come very close to
duplicating the display screen, except for

control characters which can be seen on screen but do not show up on the printed page. See also On-screen formatting.

X, Y, Z

X
The character that is entered to leave or exit from a WP to DOS. Programs such as EasyWriter and WordStar use this letter. Once Exit to DOS is carried out, any text remaining in the computer's memory will be lost. Documents should be saved before leaving the WP program. Exiting to DOS allows the user to execute other chores such as formatting a disk, backing up a file, booting another program, etc.

Zero line spacing. See Overprinting.

Zoom
A feature of some WPs which displays the format of text or graphics on the screen as it will appear in the printout. The zoom function reduces the subject matter so that it fits into the parameters of a vertical printed page.

APPENDICES

Appendix A

A Review of Twelve Word Processors

The WPs reviewed below were chosen for many reasons. The programs are readily available, often at deep discounts. Some represent the most advanced state of word processing, while others offer a surprising array of features at a moderate price. All are effective in what they are intended to do. Some are for beginners, while others are for professional writers. The most important reason they have been singled out is that each program has been around long enough to have a proven track record and a loyal following among writers in various fields. The reviews are based on the author's personal use of many of the programs, the experiences of instructors of word processing, and the frustrations and successes of students who have handled some of the WPs.

APPLE WRITER II
Apple Computer, Inc.
20525 Mariani Avenue
Cupertino, CA 95014
(408) 996-1010
System: Apple IIe
Requirements: 64K, one disk drive
Price: $195

Apple Writer II, considered by many to be one of the best word processors for the Apple IIe, sports a variety of features that make writing with a computer effortless and enjoyable. The program is easy to learn and just as easy to use. Additional features, once they are learned, help you to use shortcuts during editing and entering text, to enhance your document, and to maneuver your files quickly.

Once you enter the workspace, you find an almost blank screen except for one data line on top, which tells you the direction the program will search during the search and replace mode, the remaining memory, the length of your document, the position of the cursor, the tab position, and the file name. The rest of the screen is for text entry. If you find that even this one data line distracts you, you can temporarily remove it. Entering information is simple. A blinking cursor guides you along. Pressing Control and the letter O (for DOS commands) brings up a screen of options: A. Catalog, B. Rename File, C. Verify File, D. Lock File, E. Unlock File, F. Delete File, and G. Initialize Disk. You can retrieve these functions simply by pressing the designated letter. Most of the commands operate mnemonically with the control key: Control L for load, S for save, P for print, F for find and replace, and so on.

Cursor movement is just as easy. Control B takes you to the beginning of your text and Control E to the end. The four arrow keys move the cursor in the direction of the arrow. When you use the open Apple key with the left arrow, text is temporarily deleted and stored in a buffer; you can retrieve the characters or lines anywhere in the document by pressing Open Apple and the right arrow. The closed Apple key in combination with the up arrow jumps the cursor 12 lines up, while the down arrow key moves it 12 lines down.

The print menu produces a large list of options, including all margin settings, page number, top and bottom headers, etc. Other formatting requirements, such as line centering, can be controlled through dot commands entered into the document.

Apple Writer II offers some unique features. You can examine a file on disk without loading it into memory. You can create a glossary file, a valuable time-saving device which will hold words, sentences, and paragraphs that can be repeated anywhere in your text simply by pressing a few keys. You can underline words by placing slashes around the text. (This may not work with your printer, however, in which case you will have to enter a special code.)

There are some items missing from this otherwise excellent program. There is no facility for seeing on screen how your document will appear in print. The program offers no provisions for proportional spacing, footnotes and endnotes, or for generating tables of contents and indexes. You can right justify your document, but you can't see that on screen. At the present time, no spelling checker accompanies the software. The program, however, works so well with Apple IIe that anyone who uses this machine without Writer II is missing out on a worthwhile word processor.

BANK STREET WRITER
Broderbund Software
1938 Fourth Street
San Rafael, CA 94901
(415) 479-1170
System: Apple II Series, Atari, Commodore, IBM.
Requirements: 64K, one disk drive
Price: Apple, etc: $69.95; IBM: $79.95

Bank Street Writer is one of the simplest word processors to learn and one of the easiest to use. Developed by the Bank Street College of Education for use in the classroom, this inexpensive program has gained some popularity in the home as well. It cannot, of course, perform many of the feats of its more costly big brothers, but it holds its own for what it was designed to accomplish.

Any good word processor, regardless of its cost, should provide the basic functions expected of an electronic writing tool. Its editing features should include its ability to insert text in the middle of a word or sentence, delete text, and move text elsewhere. It should contain some method of searching for and replacing text. It should offer some type of help screen and tutorial. A format or ruler line should be displayed to inform you where you are in your document and which format features are in operation. Finally, the printing task should be relatively effortless. Bank Street Writer offers all these and more. Additional features include repeat Search and Replace, page length and width display, conditional page length, an undo command, and changeable defaults.

Bank Street Writer uses prompts for many of its functions. For instance, when you have marked a block of text for deletion, you are asked by a flashing message whether or not you want the text erased. Only after you type "Y" (for Yes) is the text removed. The print screen allows you to change defaults through a series of prompt questions, among them: "How many characters per line?," "Pages to be numbered? (Y/N)," and "Spacing between lines (1-3)?"

Other screens help you through various functions. Another menu displays nine more options: Retrieve, Delete, Print-Draft, Quit, Save, Init (initialize disk), Rename, Print-Final, and Clear. A utility menu lets you change set-up items, display passwords, convert writer files, or quit the program. Each of these is numbered, and pressing some brings up other screens and options.

Bank Street Writer comes in different versions for different machines. The program produces only 40 characters per line, so you do not see on screen how your printed page will actually look. The version for the Apple IIc, however, can handle a 40- or 80-column board. There is no facility for underlining, unfortunately; students and others could use such a feature when citing sources.

Although many other desirable features are missing--among them the ability to move the cursor to the next screen, to the end of a line, to the beginning or end of a block of text, or to the top or bottom of the screen; to delete by word, sentence, or line; to include footnotes or print boldface--Bank Street Writer serves as a good starting program for the neophyte or student, almost making writing fun.

DISPLAYWRITE
IBM
Box 1328-S
Boca Raton, FL 33432
(800) 447-4700
System: IBM
Requirements: DisplayWrite 2: DOS 2.0, 192K, two disk drives; DOS 3.0, 256K, two disk drives; DisplayWrite 3: DOS 2.0, 256K,two disk drives
Price: DisplayWrite 2: $299; DisplayWrite 3: $349

IBM's two leading word processors, DisplayWrite 2 and 3, offer many worthwhile features as well as some disappointments. Since DisplayWrite 3 is the deluxe version--it provides more choices of operations on its opening menu, produces footnotes and proportional spacing, runs faster in performing certain tasks--we will concentrate on this model in our discussion.

Two features in particular that are simpler with DisplayWrite than with other word processors in its category are its approach to block moves and its search-and-replace function. Some programs require a complex procedure for moving blocks of text, including marking the segment to be moved, saving it to disk under a separate file name, then re-entering it onto the document in memory, and, finally, removing the temporary file from the disk directory. DisplayWrite simplifies all this by applying the familiar highlighting method. All you do is place the cursor at the beginning of the passage to be moved, highlight the text to the end of the segment, and press Enter. Next, move the cursor to where you want the text to appear and simply press Enter again. Screen prompts guide you continuously. That's all there is to it.

The program's search and replace leaves other word processors at the starting gate. The function can handle three searches at the same time. A different screen is employed; and, as with the block move, a series of simple prompts carry you through the task. However, there is no provision for wildcard search or backward search.

Another worthwhile feature is Display-Write's method of saving documents. Each time you return to the main menu (by pressing the F2 function key), your document in memory is stored on disk automatically. So much for lost documents.

DisplayWrite is a four-disk, menu- and command-driven program which permits an unlimited number of backups to be made and contains a spelling checker with a dictionary of 100,000 words--one of the most comprehensive available. You can rename and copy files, use files from any subdirectory, and chain and queue documents for printing.

Its printing capabilities are about average. What you see on the screen will be printed on your hard copy. You can print part of a file and edit during printing. There are facilities for printing labels and envelopes. The program can handle sub- and superscripts as well as proportional spacing. Line spacing ranges from half-space to triple-space, not the most generous but adequate for most occasions. The printer control functions are above average, including its screen of options in which you need to enter only the number of your selection.

The program can display up to 455 characters per line--one of the highest in the industry--while producing 20 lines per screen--one of the lowest. It can create macros, redefine key functions, handle automatic hyphens, and produce multiple or single headers and footers. There is even a facility for performing math functions. The editing screen displays the line and page number.

DisplayWrite falls short in its editing features. There is no provision for moving the cursor by word, by sentence, or by paragraph, although you can move it by screen and to the beginning and end of lines as well as the entire document. Its ability to delete also leaves something to be desired. There is no procedure to erase by word, line, sentence, or paragraph. Neither is there any provision to delete to the end of a document. Needless to say, there is no undelete function.

Other shortcomings include no on-screen or textbook tutorial; no utility for generating an index or a table of contents; no procedures for editing multiple files, moving between files, backing up a file automatically, or saving a file without first exiting from the program.

If you can live with these drawbacks,

Displaywrite 3 has enough strengths to qualify it as a high-ranking program for diverse jobs around the office or the home. The slight difference in price between versions 2 and 3 make the latter the better choice; it is more responsive and offers more features for the extra few dollars.

EASYWRITER II
Sorcim/IUS
2195 Fortune Drive
San Jose, CA 95131
System: MS-DOS (IBM, etc.)
Requirements: DOS 2.0 or later, 192K, two disk drives
Price: $395

EasyWriter II's newest entry, Version 4.1, is an enhanced edition of former II models and worlds apart from the original Easy-Writer I. In fact, versions I and II are entirely different word processors. Earlier II programs were unique in that they did not run under MS-DOS or PC-DOS, the most popular disk operating systems. The most recent version, 4.1, however, operates under DOS 2.0 or more and is a full-featured package which includes a mail-merge utility and a spelling checker program.

Its main menu of possible activities include the following: 1. Edit, 2. Open File Folder, 3. Delete Document, 4. Print, 5. Paginate Document, 6. Set Date, 7. Print Document List, 8. System Functions, and 9. Extended Functions. You can select one of these options simply by typing its number. The bottom portion of the Main Menu screen lists the directory documents. File names appear in bright intensity, while other information and data are displayed in normal intensity.

Once you've selected your function and file, the excellent, uncluttered screen layout displays a data line containing line, column and page numbers, document name, system date, current mode, and the percentage of memory that is full. The ruler line appears below this data line and provides for margins, tabs, etc.

EasyWriter II is a page-oriented word processor; therefore, like MultiMate and other similar programs, it does not operate as briskly as document-oriented processors. Its text-reformatting function also is rather slow. The editing process is hampered by the lack of automatic reformatting. Each time a paragraph is altered, it has to be individually reformatted. (This is also the bane of earlier WordStar versions such as 3.2, finally corrected in WordStar 2000.)

Some general features of EasyWriter II Version 4.1 include the ability to make unlimited backup copies, an on-screen as well as a printed tutorial, a spelling checker of almost 90,000 entries, a block operation of a maximum of 50 lines defined by highlighting, and a block save function. This 50-line limit can prove a serious handicap, especially by today's standards; other programs offer anywhere from 25 pages to unlimited capacity. Also, there are no provisions to generate a table of contents or an index.

Its file-handling capabilities are average. It can rename, copy, and move between files, but it cannot edit multiple files. It can save files automatically, read DOS files, and chain and queue documents for printing. On the other hand, the program cannot use files from any subdirectory, cannot save a file without first exiting from the document, and cannot make automatic backups of files. Also, it cannot input or convert files from WordStar, a small inconvenience. Neither can it exchange disks during the editing process, another minor point.

There are some strengths and some shortcomings in terms of printing features. What you see on screen is what will be printed. You can edit during printing, print part of a file (by page only), and print envelopes and labels. But you cannot print multiple copies or print without first saving the file. You can print sub- and superscripts, but proportional spacing is unavailable. Line-spacing options range from single- to triple-space, not a very generous offering but adequate for most purposes. Multiple-column printing is unlimited.

The editing functions are more than sufficient. You can move the cursor by word, sentence, paragraph, or screen. You can delete by word, line, sentence, or paragraph. You cannot, however, delete to the end of the document, presumably because of its page-oriented set-up. Also, there is no undelete function. You can move and copy columns of text. The search-and-replace feature works fairly well, offering backward search as well as the ability to ignore case during the search process. The search feature, however, is very slow. There is no wildcard search.

EasyWriter II can handle 255 characters per line and displays 22 lines per screen, both average for its price range. Hyphenation is very flexible; you have the option of automatic hyphenation, hard hyphens or soft. Multiple headers and footers can be inserted into text. Also, multiple indents and outdents are featured.

This is a solid word processor with many advanced features. However, it tends to operate slowly in many areas. It is one of the slowest in its price range in terms of moving blocks of text, in searching through text, in appending one file to the end of another (requiring an inordinate number of keystrokes), and in reformatting a file. It does score high in its speed at sending a document to a printer, in storing the document and exiting to DOS, and in retrieving certain files from disk

to screen. If you can overlook its lack of
speed in some areas and its page-oriented
system, this word processor can be a valuable
tool.

MICROSOFT WORD
Microsoft Corporation
10700 Northup Way
Bellevue, WA 98009
(206) 828-8080
System: MS-DOS (IBM, etc.); Macintosh
Requirements: DOS 2.0 or later, 192K, two disk
drives; 128K with Macintosh
Price: $375

   Long recognized for its flexibility and
dexterity, Microsoft's Word shines because of
its special features. Some of these are minor
ones, but they add up to a solid program which
can handle various jobs well, with a proficiency not often found in other similar packages. Word has one version for PC machines and
another for the Macintosh. Each works smoothly
and offers some different features because of
the nature of each computer.
   The PC version offers easy access to its
editing and formatting functions through its
menus and submenus or through the keyboard.
Using the keyboard gets you where you want to
go faster, but it is more difficult to learn
the many combinations. Using the program's
menu-driven approach, therefore, may be easier
for the beginner. By the way, the excellent
on-screen tutor, complete with graphics, can
have you operating the program in just a few
hours.
   Although Word lets you select from monochrome, color, or special graphics in the
booting process, the operation is slower than
most programs in its category. The booting,
however, allows you to load a file automatically. The file can be the last document you

263

edited or another of your choice. Word makes a half-hearted attempt to use mnenonics for some of its functions: L for Load, T for calling up the transfer menu, M for Merge, and so on.

The program allows you to make just two backup copies of the program. This should be enough to hold you, but the company is not as generous as others that permit unlimited back-ups. Installing Word takes about one hour, a little longer than most programs. The spelling checker has a dictionary of 80,000 words, includes many proper nouns such as cities and states, and operates directly from the menu. Unfortunately, there is no provision for generating a table of contents or an index.

The file-handling capabilities are above average. You can edit two different files, move between them with ease, and rename them. You can save a file without exiting from the program, use files from any subdirectory, and exchange disks during editing. The program permits you to chain or queue your documents for printing purposes.

Speaking of printing, Word supports more than 50 machines as well as the new laser printers. What you see on the screen is what you get on the hard copy. You can edit the same document during printing, print part of a file, print without saving the document, print sub- and superscripts as well as labels and envelopes, and print an unlimited number of multiple columns. The only function you can't perform is printing multiple copies. Word handles proportional spacing, footnotes and endnotes, and line spacing from single-space to 132 spaces.

Word provides a generous supply of writing functions. You can create macros and redefine key functions. Other offerings include various hyphen options, automatic indentation, automatic paragraph reformatting, and multiple indents and outdents.

The editing features are not as generous.

Although you can move the cursor by word or screen, you cannot move it by sentence or paragraph. Deletions fare slightly better. You can erase by word, sentence, and paragraph, but not by line. You can, however, delete to the end of your document. The search-and-replace feature is flexible and works faster than most of the competition.

Microsoft Word for the Macintosh takes advantage of scroll bars, pull-down menus, and the crafty mouse. Word offers an excellent merge capability and glossary feature. Fonts can be changed through keyboard commands or through a dialog box, the latter being a more efficient approach, especially with character font, position, and size.

Other tasks such as left, right, and full justification, line centering, additions of lines before or after paragraphs, and various indentations are performed with equal nimbleness. Pictures created with the MacPaint program and charts made with Microsoft's Chart software can be transferred into a Word document. Footers, headers, and repagination are controlled by the document menu. Footers and headers are not restricted to any size and they can be numbered automatically or used with a preset symbol. When a footnote is added or removed, the numbers re-adjust automatically.

A vast array of commands can be operated by the use of keyboard sequences. Although Apple does not provide any cursor control keys (leaving this task to its mouse), Word rectifies this by offering a group of keys in a diamond layout for moving the cursor. As you can see, Microsoft took pains to present a useful, comprehensive program.

Word tends to operate much more quickly on the Macintosh than it does on the PC and is superior to MacWrite, another word processor designed for the Macintosh. The program seems to be a perfect match for Macintosh, especial-

ly in relation to the visual effectiveness of
its screen.

Regardless of the machine with which Word
is used, it performs well under most conditions. Its newest version, 2.0, offers an
updated dictionary, improved documentation,
and support for laser technology and the concept of the mouse. The combination of Word and
its special character formats with a laser
printer produces results that are truly out-
standing. The program has some weaknesses, but
its strengths far outweigh these. It may prove
difficult at first to learn all the keyboard
commands, but once the keys are learned, the
user will appreciate the power of Word.

MULTIMATE
MultiMate International Corporation
52 Oakland Avenue North
East Hartford, CT 06108
(203) 522-2116
System: MS-DOS (IBM, etc.)
Requirements: DOS 1.1 or later, 256K, two disk
drives
Price: $495

MultiMate is basically a command-oriented
word processor with many advanced features.
Although a few menus are available, anyone
wishing to become proficient in this program
must learn hundreds of commands. It is also
page-oriented; only one page of text is stored
in memory at a time. During searches, Multi-
Mate reads and writes to disk each page. As
you can see by this process, page-oriented
systems are generally slower than document-
oriented ones. One of its advantages, however,
is its saving capability; if things go wrong,
you cannot lose more than one page of text.

The program can merge documents, recall
text, locate a specific page of a document
with relatively few keystrokes, check spell-

ing, program keys, and perform many other sophisticated word processing tasks.

The concept of MultiMate emerged from the Wang dedicated word processing system. This accounts for its many strong points. Keys that operate many of its functions have a logical arrangement; block moves and merging capabilities are fast and efficient; and its list of other features seems endless. Among these are search and replace, alignment of numbers and text by either comma or decimal point, horizontal and vertical column addition and subtraction, column insertion, storage of frequently used keystroke sequences, creation of key procedures, the ability to change system defaults, document recovery, and document conversion.

After booting, you are presented with a main menu consisting of nine choices: 1) Edit an Old Document, 2) Create a New Document, 3) Print Document, 4) Printer Control, 5) Merge Print Utilities, 6) Document Handling Utilities, 7) Other Utilities, 8) Spell Check a Document, and 9) Return to DOS. While in the main menu mode, you can call up the help menu by pressing Shift and F1. The help menu can also be viewed while editing a document.

A unique feature is the document summary screen. This appears on screen once you select a file. Its purpose is to help you keep a record of a document so that you can review significant facts without reading the whole document. The summary screen prompts you to supply such information as document name, author, operator, identification of key words, creation and modification date, and so on. Near the lower part of the screen a few lines allow you to enter comments. The document summary screen can be printed along with the document. All you have to do is press Y. This data screen can prove useful with long documents such as chapters of a book, articles, and extensive reports.

Some file-handling features include its ability to rename, copy, and move between files; to use files from any subdirectory; to save files automatically; and to queue documents for printing.

MultiMate excels in printing capabilities. What you see on the screen is what you get on the printed page. You can edit during printing, print part of a line, print without saving, and print multiple copies. Pages are numbered automatically. You can print sub- and superscripts, opt for proportional spacing, enter embedded codes, print envelopes, and change print wheels while in the pause mode. Its line-spacing facility is one of the most flexible available. It can be set anywhere from single space to 132 spaces between lines. MultiMate supports almost 300 printers. For those with unsupported printers, printer action tables permit you to add modifications, a very practical consideration for users with special printer problems.

Its writing features fall between average and slightly above average. Multimate can handle 150 characters per line (the typical range for word processors in its category is from 80 to 455), while displaying 22 lines per screen (again, the average is 22 to 23). It provides automatic indentation as well as multiple indents/outdents. Paragraph reformatting is not required--a definite advantage. The display line includes column, line, and page number; page breaks are also displayed on screen. The program does not provide automatic hyphens or the redefinition of key functions, minor inconveniences.

MultiMate can move the cursor by word and by screen, but not by sentence or paragraph. The cursor can be moved to the beginning or the end of a screen, but not to the start or end of a document. Other editing functions include deletion by word, line, sentence, and paragraph. You cannot delete to the end of a document and there is no undelete feature.

This is certainly a powerful package, but it does have some drawbacks. It cannot generate a table of contents or an index, save a block of text, or edit multiple files. Finally, although the program saves the current document by page, there is no provision for an automatic backup file.

Three different versions of MultiMate are available. Versions 3.3 and 3.4 (the most recent entry) are the most popular and are similar in their features. MultiMate 3.2, the old standard, seems to have been superseded by the others. Any one of these will provide a high-quality word processor for the home or office. MultiMate may have some shortcomings, as does every word handler, but its strengths outweigh its weaknesses. It is consistently ranked among the top five or 10 programs.

PFS: WRITE
Software Publishing Corporation
1901 Landings Drive
Mountain Drive, CA 94043
(415) 962-8910
System: DOS 3.3 (Apple IIe, etc.); MS-DOS
(IBM and compatibles)
Requirements: Apple: DOS 3.3, 64K, one disk
drive; IBM: DOS 1.1 or later, 128K,
one disk drive
Price: $140

PFS: Write is an inexpensive, uncompli-cated word processing program that is easy to learn and use. Its ease stems from the fact that it is menu- rather than command-driven. To perform most tasks, you simply call on the proper menu. Granted, it does not offer the sophisticated features of the more profes-sional packages, but it can tackle many jobs around the home or office with little effort.

The program has been designed in two versions, one for the Apple machine and the other for the PC computer. Both have similar features, the one exception being its utilization of the 10 function keys with the PC version. We will devote this review to the use of the Apple IIe with PFS: Write.

The main menu offers five options: 1. Type/Edit, 2. Define Page, 3. Print, 4. Get/Save/Remove, and 5. Clear. To engage any of these functions, you simply type the correct number. The first lets you edit a new document or one already stored on disk. The second helps you enter your margins, headings, and footings. The print option permits you to specify line spacing (single or double) and the number of copies you wish to print, as well as direct the actual printing. The fourth is more or less self-explanatory--except that Remove is different from the fifth choice, Clear. The former permanently deletes a file from the disk, while the latter erases a document from the screen and memory.

Software Publishing was clever in its selection of which features to include and which to omit. Publishing an inexpensive word processor puts great demands on its designers. But Software was practical in including on-screen help (retrieved by using the open apple and H keys), a block move and edit function (using highlighting), underlining (pressing Control and _) and boldface display (typing Control and B), and on-screen formatting which lets you see exactly what will be printed. Text marked for underlining and boldface is highlighted on screen.

The workspace is not only uncluttered, it is practically bare except for a bottom bar which specifies the page and line number as well as the percentage of memory consumed. The screen resembles a blank sheet of paper set in a typewriter, complete with top and side margins. This is a definite advantage for beginners, who may be intimidated by other word processors with main editing screens filled with all kinds of arcane functions and commands. If you need assistance, a help screen appears almost instantaneously with an array of cursor commands and editing functions. The program attempts to use mnemonics for almost all of its commands, except for Insert, which requires that the Control and Y keys be pressed.

PFS: Write lets you scroll by line, make one back-up copy, and move blocks of text of up to 100 lines. You are limited to a document size of about 20 pages. You can use files from any subdirectory, save a document without exiting from the program, and exchange disks during editing. You can print part of a document page by page only, print without saving a document, and print labels and envelopes.

The cursor can be moved by word or by screen as well as to the beginning and end of a line or document. Deletions are by word and line only. The search-and-replace function, which includes a wildcard search, works well but is rather limited in its ability to search backward or ignore case--minor inconveniences. The program offers headers and footers, but has no facility for footnotes and endnotes.

Although PFS: Write is more than a no-frills program, it lacks the advanced features of its big cousins. This is not a professional word processor by any means, and does not make that claim. But it acts as a good workhorse around the home and office for small jobs and is excellent as a second word processor in any environment. It is highly recommended with these uses in mind.

SAMNA WORD III
Samna Corporation
2700 NE Expressway, #C700
Atlanta, GA 30345
(404) 321-5006
System: MS-DOS (IBM, etc.)
Requirements: DOS 2.0 or later, 256K, two disk
drives
Price: $550

Samna Word III is an expensive, but interesting, screen-oriented word processor that
offers multiple formats, multiple levels of
on-screen help, underlining and boldface right
on the screen, and character pitch alterations
while you are working on your document.
The five-disk package allows you to make
up to two back-up copies, contains an excellent on-screen tutorial (no textbook version),
and provides a built-in spelling checker. It
is a command-driven program which can generate
tables of contents and indexes and save blocks
of text. (However, the maximum size of the
block operation is restricted to a paragraph.)
Its command-driven orientation deserves some
study. Although this type of approach, in
contrast to menu-driven programs, operates
much faster, it can be burdensome to learn. To
work the program efficiently, you should learn
as many of the function commands as possible.
This can be time-consuming for the average
user and quite difficult for the beginner.
It handles files rather capably. The size
of the document is limited only by the disk
capacity. The program is document- rather than
page-oriented; this can be a definite advantage, especially if you work with long files
such as articles and chapters of a book. You
can edit two different files simultaneously,
copy files, move between files, use files from
any subdirectory, and save a document without

first having to exit from the program. Samna Word also permits you to change disks during the editing process and chain and queue documents for printing purposes. It offers you the option of backing up your files automatically. You cannot convert WordStar files or save your working file automatically.

Samna Word III excels in its printing capabilities, although some tasks seem to take longer than necessary. This becomes obvious once you compare it to other similar programs. What appears on screen will appear in print, including on-screen underlining, a feature not found in many programs. You can print multiple columns and part of a file, edit during printing, print multiple copies, and print without first having to save the document. The program can handle automatic page numbering, sub- and superscripts, and proportional spacing. There is a facility for printing labels and envelopes as well as footnotes and endnotes. There is no pause for entering text, but there is one for changing the print wheel. Line spacing ranges from half-space to four spaces between lines of text. There is no provision for entering embedded control codes. Almost 30 printers are supported, with allowances for other machines through special printer utilities.

All 10 function keys can be redefined, macros can be created, and some hyphen functions are provided. Samna also offers automatic indentation, multiple or single headers and footers, math functions, and multiple indents and outdents. Paragraph reformatting, although painfully slow, is automatic. The on-screen workspace displays column, line, and page number. Page break displays are optional.

Editing functions are fairly extensive. But one oddity is its lack of a toggle for inserting and/or overwriting text. This is one of the few word processors to omit this feature. The cursor can be controlled by word, sentence, or paragraph. It can be moved to the beginning or end of a line, screen, or document. You can delete text in many ways: by word, line, sentence, paragraph, or to the end of a document. There is an undelete feature. The search-and-replace function offers various options, but there is no wildcard search. Another weakness here is that Search and Replace is very slow.

Samna Word III is a highly respected program, especially among writers who need many of its special features. It can be a very useful tool for secretaries who work with only a few pages of text at a time and for those who need a program that can handle longer reports. Because of its relatively high price, it is recommended more for the office than for the home. Its few faults--user difficulty in learning all its functions and its slow operation in performing many tasks, to mention a few--may dissuade some users from purchasing the Samna. But its strengths make it a serious contender among worthy word processors.

VOLKSWRITER DELUXE
Lifetree Software
411 Pacific Street, #315
Monterey, CA 93940
(408) 659-3221
System: MS-DOS (IBM, etc.)
Requirements: DOS 1.1 or later, 128K, two disk drives
Price: $295

Originally, Volkswriter was one of the best word processors on the market, supported by many publishing houses. However, other companies have surpassed this program by offering more advanced features and quicker responses in some areas. This has forced Volkswriter to come out with an enhanced, deluxe version.

274

Features include extensive cursor control, the standard editing and formatting functions, on-screen help, file size dependent upon disk capacity, automatic back-up of files, on-screen formatting which displays your document exactly as it will appear in print, mail-merge capability, embedded print commands, and support for a wide array of printers. The program is not copy-protected, allowing you to make as many archival copies as you need.

The search and replace feature works equally fast compared with other word processors. On the bottom line you are offered prompts for replacing words. Various options such as global search can be achieved by a simple yes-or-no choice. Moving a block of text is handled in average time, but appending one file to another is accomplished very quickly. Printing a document to a disk file is accomplished with extreme speed. However, the package does not do so well in transmitting a document to the printer. Other programs are much faster.

The uncluttered main menu offers you a choice of 12 options, each of which can be gotten by typing in the first letter. For example, typing D (for Display All Files) brings up the directory to the screen. The program makes effective use of the function keys. F8, for instance, is used to reformat a paragraph, F2 with the alternate key is employed during the file merge process, and so on.

The program is menu-oriented as well as command-driven. The menus are clearly displayed and helpful. The commands allow the processor to work quickly and efficiently. An advantage of this dual set-up is that you can select whichever method is convenient for you at the moment; you can call up a command or select a function from the menu.

Other features include a block save function and block operations with unlimited text size. Files can be saved without exiting from the program as well as renamed and copied. Automatic backup of a file is optional. Documents can be chained but not queued for printing.

The number of printing features available is above average for a word processor in this price range. You can edit during printing, print without saving the document in memory, print labels and envelopes, print sub- and superscripts and multiple columns. Line-spacing offers a wide range--from single-space to 66 lines. The program supports more than 30 printers with utilities for accepting other machines.

Many editing features are provided. You can move the cursor by word or by screen, as well as to the beginning and end of the screen and document. Deletions are by word and line only. Columns can be copied or moved.

Volkswriter has a few drawbacks. There is no spelling checker built into the word processor. Tables of contents and indexes cannot be generated. There is no provision for editing multiple files. Files cannot be copied or automatically saved, and multiple copies cannot be printed. Once again, as in other word processors, formatting proves to be the weakest point of the program. Reformatting each and every paragraph becomes a burdensome chore. The fundamentals are easy to learn, but its advanced features are difficult to remember. Some formatting features work rather awkwardly.

However, one should not be dissuaded from considering this heavy-duty package because of a few faults. Volkwriter Deluxe has some very good points: The program works fast, has a generous help menu, contains some advanced features, and uses relatively few keystrokes for many of its commands. It can be very effective in meeting general writing needs.

WORDSTAR
Micropro International Corporation
33 San Pablo Avenue
San Rafael, CA 94903
(415) 499-1200
System: MS-DOS (IBM, etc.); CP/M with Apple,
etc.
Requirements: 96K minimum, 192K with
SpellStar; DOS 1.1 or later; one disk drive
Price: $495

The legendary WordStar word processor has
been around now for a few years and has become
one of the most popular programs in use today.
Its success may have been due to the lack of
competition, but this powerful workhorse has
many functions and special features, making it
a desirable choice for users in various
fields.

The program contains the usual functions
one expects from today's state-of-the-art word
processor. It can automatically number pages;
set margins; handle underlining, boldface,
sub- and superscripts, and other similar
chores, as long as the printer has these capabilities.

Once the program is booted up, the screen
displays an opening menu and a directory of
programs on disk. From this menu you can print
a document, edit a file, or create a new one.
You can also rename a file or copy or delete
one. The menu also permits you to use optional
features such as MailMerge and SpellStar, a
spelling checker. WordStar has so many commands that neophytes can easily become intimidated or confused, but learning these can
prove very useful in the long run.

One of the problems with WordStar is that
the commands are not mnemonic and seem to make
little sense. For example, to delete a line
you have to press the Control key and the

letter Y. To save a document to disk you press Control and K, then D. However, many of these commands appear on the various menus which remain constantly on the screen in reverse video, occupying about one-third of the working area. Once you become familiar with the various commands, you can remove these help screens.

One important feature of any word processor is its ability to move blocks of text. WordStar can perform this task, but it does so in a rather clumsy manner. The text must first be "marked" at the beginning of the passage and at the end, then written to a disk, again using Control K (for Block) and W. The program then prompts you for a new file name. The block of text can then be recalled with Control K and R (for Read) and added to another segment of the document or a different document. Later, you must delete these short documents or your disk will become cluttered with a group of block files, meaningless documents once their original purpose has been served.

The search-and-replace function works smoothly, as do the save and load commands, the margin settings, and the page breaks. There are two modes for saving text. One allows you to save your material while editing, keeping the document on screen so that you can continue to work on it; the other mode places you back with the main menu ready to print or go to another document. The margins and page breaks can be adjusted before you begin a document or when a document is completed. Line spacing, however, should be selected before any work is begun, since it is formatted on screen. In other words, if you select double-space, text will appear on the screen with every other line blank. But if you decide to change your mind and want to convert to single space, you must put in some additional work and time, an inconvenience with long documents such as a chapter of a book. The on-screen line formatting can be a useful tool, since it can help in previewing how a document will look on the page. It also gives you an accurate page count.

Some annoying aspects of WordStar include its automatic justification, automatic page numbering, and manual reformatting, which is required each time you edit a paragraph or line of text. If you don't want the right justification default setting, you can disconnect the toggle by hitting Control O and J. To omit page numbers, you will have to enter dot commands into your text; e.g., .OP must be placed at the extreme left margin. The most inconvenient function is paragraph reformatting. When you enter or delete text that alters a line, you must return to the beginning of that paragraph and press Control B; this reformats the paragraph so that it conforms to the preset margins. There are other word processors which automatically reformat text which has been edited.

Some excellent features of WordStar include its speed, especially when used with a hard disk drive; its use of the special function keys on IBM-type keyboards; its wide array of help levels; its column-move capability; and its on-screen formatting. The last feature lets you see how the printed document will finally look. Special printing function symbols, such as those used for underlining and boldface, appear on screen but do not affect the way the document will appear in print.

WordStar is a professional program recommended for those who want a word processor which can handle complex as well as basic tasks. It will take a long time before the user outgrows all its functions and features. Although it is difficult to learn, it is easy to use once the commands and the control keys become familiar.

WORDSTAR 2000
Micropro International Corporation
33 San Pablo Avenue
San Rafael, CA 94903
(415) 499-1200
System: MS-DOS (IBM, etc.)
Requirements: DOS 2.0 or later, 256K; DOS 3.0,
320K; two drives
Price: $495

WordStar 2000, a relatively recent entry,
seems to have been designed for those who
liked the classic WordStar program but found
its shortcomings too numerous and too bother-
some to adapt to. Micropro was determined to
keep or regain these users within its family
by eliminating many of the disadvantages of
the original program while adding a few new
features. The new version, for instance, permits the user to print multiple copies, provides proportional spacing, replaces the dot
commands with simpler key commands, and offers
automatic reformatting of paragraphs, probably
the most wished-for change by WordStar aficio-
nados.
Other important features include the
ability to make unlimited backup copies, an
on-screen tutorial, a built-in spelling checker with a dictionary of more than 70,000
words, on-line help, a table-of-contents and
index generator, an unlimited text-size block
move, an envelope printing facility, and the
capability to print a document without first
saving it. WordStar 2000 has retained many of
the more important and familiar functions of
its namesake, such as the ability to copy
files, to save files without exiting from the
program, to suppress menus from appearing on
screen, to make automatic back-ups of files,
to view the document exactly as it will appear
in print, to number pages automatically, and
others.

Some new features are worth examining more closely. The remove command, for example, allows you to delete text by sentence, by paragraph, or from the cursor to any selected character. The undo command can recall your last deletion, a very practical feature which will surely be applied often by the average user. WordStar 2000 also has the capacity to store the formatting parameters along with the document. Another deluxe feature is a sorting utility to help you put various lists in alphabetical order. The program also includes a four-function math calculator. Boldface and underlining appear on screen, while other printing functions show up in boldface. If you are fortunate enough to have a color monitor, these functions appear in different colors. Finally, you are given the opportunity to open windows. Up to three files can be opened at one time, allowing information to be moved from one document to another.

Once the program is booted, you are presented with an opening menu which includes 12 choices: Edit/Create, Remove, Print, Copy, Get help, Quit, Directory/Drive, Move/Rename, Spelling correction, Key glossary, Typewriter mode, and Format design. A second phase of the opening menu presents an additional four choices: Access Telemerge, WS/WS 2000 file conversion, MailList, and Indexing. Any of these functions can be activated by pressing a single mnemonic key, a definite improvement over the old WordStar. The opening menu, as well as others, is less cluttered than those of the original program, another clear improvement.

The editing capabilities of WordStar 2000 earn an average rating. There is not too much that is new or surprising here. The cursor can be moved by word, screen and line, but not by sentence or paragraph. You can delete a word, a line, a sentence, a paragraph, to the end of a document. You can search backward, but there is no wildcard search.

WordStar 2000 is not without its shortcomings. All of the special features mentioned above are attained at a price. The program is much slower in some areas than its predecessor. Booting the directory of an alternate drive, for example, takes longer with 2000. Scrolling presents another problem. The screen tends to blank out, causing you to pause during scrolling so that you can find your place. Moving blocks of text with the new version is also a slower process than with the traditional WordStar. But these differences can be counted in seconds, and are not a serious detriment. Curiously, the program has no automatic indentation; function keys cannot be redefined; files cannot be saved automatically; and documents cannot be queued for printing. Again, these are minor inconveniences and in many cases they can be gotten around by using another approach. For example, the last item can be overcome by chaining documents for printing. In other words, a few chapters of a book can be joined into one long file and printed.

In general, WordStar 2000 is an exceptional program sporting many advanced features. It can help the professional writer, the serious word processing user, and those who prefer a full-featured package that will handle many different chores. The menus are easy to read and follow, the documentation is very good, the program is relatively easy to learn and easy to use. It is a clear improvement over its predecessor in most ways. It offers more than other programs in its price category, but falls short of some in terms of bug-free performance. Is it the last word in word processing? Unfortunately, the answer is "no." However, it is worth considering if you want to purchase only one word processor. Although it is more costly than some, you are getting more for your money.

XYWRITE II
XyQuest, Inc.
P.O. Box 372
Bedford, MA 01730
(617) 275-7194
System: MS-DOS (IBM, etc.)
Requirements: DOS 1.0 or later, 128K, one disk
drive
Price: $295

XyWrite II is a strong contender among
word processing programs. Its many features--
flexible formatting, advanced editing capabilities, text display options, embedded commands, and moderate price--make it an attractive alternative to the more costly processors
which have dominated the field during the last
few years.
The program is screen-oriented and command-driven. Instead of menus, you are given
an almost blank screen and a host of commands
which you must memorize to drive the editing,
printing, and most other functions. You are
not even offered a print menu, since all the
controls are embedded into the document. The
display screen contains a command line, a
message line, and a ruler across the top.
XyWrite works swiftly. Moving from the
beginning to the end of a document or paging
up and down is practically instantaneous. In
fact, it is one of the fastest processors in
its class, especially in performing the following functions: calling up an average-size
file from disk to screen, operating the
search-and-replace feature, moving a block of
text, appending one file onto the end of a
document presently on screen, reformatting
margins, printing an entire document to a
disk, and sending a document to the printer.
For example, to reformat a merged file
you need to change the margin settings and

insert indentations. With other word processors this often requires an excessive number of keystrokes and consumes a lot of time. But with XyWrite II you can perform this task with a minimum of strokes. In contrast, other programs usually take longer to accomplish the same job and with up to 10 times the number of keystrokes! Such is the speed and power of this package.

Another reason XyWrite II operates so quickly is that your document is stored in RAM (Random Access Memory). There is hardly any toggling back and forth between the disk and the computer memory while the editing process is in progress. Because you don't have to sit around waiting for the program to restore itself, you can continue entering and editing your document. This can be a real time-saver.

Because there are no menus, all functions such as search-and-replace and margin settings are controlled from the command line mentioned earlier. For example, to change margin settings during reformatting, all you have to do is enter RM 65 and the right margin changes; type in IP5 for indentations of all first lines of paragraphs and they will all be indented five spaces. This completes the reformatting. Try this with processors such as WordStar or MultiMate and see how long this operation takes. You, too, will join the many converts to XyWrite.

Other features include the ability to generate tables of contents and indexes, to save blocks of text, and to manipulate blocks of text of unlimited size. You can move between files, save a file without exiting from the program, exchange disks during editing, and use files from any subdirectory. You are even given an option to back up files automatically if you prefer.

The printing features are somewhat above average for word processors in this category. What you see on the screen is what you will get when your document is printed. You can edit during printing, print a document in memory without having to first save it, and print part of a file (from one page number to another). The program offers automatic page numbering, sub- and superscripts, proportional spacing, footnotes and endnotes, and accepts embedded controls. The line-spacing feature is more than sufficient, allowing you to select from single-space to nine spaces. The program supports 33 different printers and has utilities for accepting other printers.

However, there are some shortcomings in the area of printing. XyWrite does not allow for printing multiple copies, labels or envelopes, or multiple columns. Also, there is no provision for pausing during the printing process for the purpose of entering text. These are negligible drawbacks.

XyWrite II produces 255 characters per line and 22 lines per screen, about average for its class. There are facilities for creating macros, for automatic indentation (discussed above), and for multiple indents and outdents. You can insert multiple headers and footers into your document. The program even provides for math functions.

The editing features are quite extensive. The cursor can be moved by word, sentence, paragraph, and screen. It can be moved to the beginning and end of a line, a screen, or an entire document. Deletion capabilities are just as generous. You can delete by word, line, sentence, paragraph, or to the end of a document. There is an undelete feature in case you err from time to time. The search-and-replace feature is very flexible. It offers backward search, the ability to ignore case during a search, and a wildcard search.

It is not difficult to see from the above why XyWrite II is regarded as a word processor to reckon with. Its power and speed make it a serious choice for a wide range of users--from secretaries who type one- or two-page letters, to those who work with lengthier reports, and to professional writers who need the additional features. Its disadvantages, such as having to learn all the commands and no on-screen tutorial, are few, but worth considering before making a final decision.

Appendix B

Sources for Further Reading

Books

Anderton, Craig. Seven Simple Steps to Buying a Word Processor. New York: Warner Books, 1982.

Casady, Mona. Word/Information Processing Concepts. Cincinnati, OH: South-Western Publishing, 1984.

Cecil, Paula B. Word Processing in the Modern Office. Menlo Park, CA: The Benjamin/ Cummings Publishing Company, 1980.

Jong, Steven F. Word Processors for Small Businesses. Indianapolis, IN: Howard W. Sams and Company, 1983.

McCabe, Helen M., and Popham, Estelle L. Word Processing. New York: Harcourt, Brace, Jovanovich, 1977.

McCunn, Donald H. Write, Edit, and Print: Word Processing with Personal Computers. San Francisco: Design Enterprises of San Francisco, 1982.

McManus, Steven, and Sciven, Michael. How to Buy a Word Processor. Sherman Oaks, CA: Alfred Publishing, 1982.

McWilliams, Peter. The Word Processing Book. New York: Ballantine Books, 1982.

Meroney, John W. Word Processing Applications
    in Practice. Cincinnati, OH: South-
    Western Publishing, 1984.
Stultz, R.A. The Word Processing Handbook.
    Englewood Cliffs, NJ: Prentice-Hall,
    1982.
Zinsser, William. Writing with a Word
    Processor. New York: Harper & Row, 1983.

Software Directories

International Directory of Software.
    Princeton, NJ: Computing Publications.
    Updated quarterly.
Microcomputer Software Directory. Princeton,
    NJ: Computing Publications. Updated
    annually.
PC Clearinghouse Software Directory. Fairfax,
    VA: PC Clearinghouse. Updated annually.
Software Catalog. New York: Elsevier Science
    Publishing. Updated periodically.
Software Reports. Carlsbad, CA: Allenbach
    Industries. Published semi-annually.
TESS: The Educational Software Selector. New
    York: Teachers College Press. Updated
    periodically.
Vanlove's Apple II/III and IBM Software
    Directories. Fairfax, VA: PC Telemart,
    1984.
Whole Earth Software Review. Sausalito, CA:
    Whole Earth Publications. Published
    quarterly.

Periodicals

A+: The Independent Guide for Apple Computing,
    New York: Ziff-Davis Publishing Co.
Byte, Peterborough, NH: McGraw-Hill.

Compute!, Greensboro, NC: Compute!
        Publications.
Computer Shopper, Titusville, FL: Computer
        Shopper, Inc.
Digest of Software Reviews, Fresno, CA: School
        and Home Courseware, Inc.
Interface, Santa Cruz, CA: Mitchell
        Publishing, Inc.
Microcomputer Digest, Old Bridge, NJ:
        Microcomputer Digest, Inc.
Microcomputers in Education, Fairfield, CT:
        Queue, Inc.
New in Computing Magazine, Milwaukee, WI:
        Computer Education Services.
Nibble, Lincoln, MA: MicroSPARC, Inc.
PC Magazine, New York: Ziff-Davis Publishing
        Company.
PC World, San Francisco: PC World
        Communications.
Personal Computing, Hasbrouck Heights, NJ:
        Hayden Publishing.

The camera-ready pages for this book
were prepared on a Tandy 1200 HD computer
using a WordStar 3.3 word processor
and a Juki 6300 daisywheel printer.